A Concise Introduction
to Mixed Methods Research

This book is dedicated to Isabel Bickett Marshall (1914–2014),
who raised me as a child, and who provided love, support, and a
heightened sense of organization to my life and for my professional work.

—JWC

A Concise Introduction to Mixed Methods Research

John W. Creswell
University of Nebraska–Lincoln

Los Angeles | London | New Delhi
Singapore | Washington DC

Los Angeles | London | New Delhi
Singapore | Washington DC

FOR INFORMATION:

SAGE Publications, Inc.
2455 Teller Road
Thousand Oaks, California 91320
E-mail: order@sagepub.com

SAGE Publications Ltd.
1 Oliver's Yard
55 City Road
London EC1Y 1SP
United Kingdom

SAGE Publications India Pvt. Ltd.
B 1/I 1 Mohan Cooperative Industrial Area
Mathura Road, New Delhi 110 044
India

SAGE Publications Asia-Pacific Pte. Ltd.
3 Church Street
#10-04 Samsung Hub
Singapore 049483

Printed in the United States of America

Library of Congress Cataloging-in-Publication Data

Creswell, John W., author.

A concise introduction to mixed methods research / John W. Creswell, University of Nebraska-Lincoln.

pages cm
Includes bibliographical references.

ISBN 978-1-4833-5904-5 (pbk. : alk. paper)
1. Mixed methods research. 2. Social sciences—Research—Methodology. 3. Research—Methodology. I. Title.

H62.C69618 2015
001.4′2—dc23   2014007517

This book is printed on acid-free paper.

Acquisitions Editor: Vicki Knight
Assistant Editor: Katie Guarino
Editorial Assistant: Jessica Miller
Production Editor: Olivia Weber-Stenis
Copy Editor: Rachel Keith
Typesetter: C&M Digitals (P) Ltd.
Proofreader: Jennifer Grubba
Indexer: Michael Ferreira
Cover Designer: Candice Harman
Marketing Manager: Nicole Elliott

SUSTAINABLE FORESTRY INITIATIVE
Certified Chain of Custody
Promoting Sustainable Forestry
www.sfiprogram.org
SFI-01268

SFI label applies to text stock

14 15 16 17 18 10 9 8 7 6 5 4 3 2 1

CONTENTS

PREFACE

I assume that in reading this book you are interested in exploring or maybe conducting mixed methods research. Also, I assume that you probably have a research problem or question which can be best answered by collecting and analyzing both quantitative (e.g., survey) and qualitative (e.g., interview) data. Did you know that bringing the two together (e.g., mixing) adds value to a study and enables you to understand your problem and questions better than simply reporting survey results and interview results separately? When you bring them together, then, how will you combine the two databases when one consists of numbers (survey data) and the other words (interview data). How can your study be presented as a good research project? Welcome to this book! You will learn how to bring the two together and, moreover, frame your "mixing" of methods in a rigorous, systematic way for publication and potential funding.

❖ PURPOSE OF THE BOOK

The idea for this book originated from my work over the last 10 to 15 years, providing workshops on mixed methods research. These workshops have been largely aimed at beginning mixed methods researchers—graduate students seeking to develop a thesis or dissertation using mixed methods, or faculty or researchers developing proposals for funding containing this methodology. The approach I have taken has been to invite participants to bring a mixed methods project they would like to work on during the workshop. This approach has seemed to work well, but I have often thought that our work together would be enhanced if participants had some background in mixed methods to build on. Unfortunately, although there are approximately 31 books devoted primarily or exclusively to mixed methods (Onwuegbuzie, 2012), many are long treatises on the subject—including the one I coauthored with Vicki Plano Clark (Creswell & Plano Clark, 2011), which stretches for 347 pages. Many workshop participants simply do not have time to read these long books or even to devote time to finding and reading shorter chapters on mixed methods in research methods books (Creswell, 2012). They may also not have time to locate and read journal articles on how to conduct mixed methods research. I felt there was a need for a concise book that would introduce my workshop participants to mixed methods and take only about two to three hours to read. The main purpose of this book is to provide an overview of mixed methods research, and to take the reader through the essential steps in planning or designing a study. As a concise book, it will not be an extensive treatment of mixed methods. It should, however, provide a foundation for understanding the methodology.

AUDIENCE

This concise introduction to mixed methods research is geared toward the beginner in mixed methods or the more advanced researcher who needs a quick refresher on mixed methods. It should provide this introduction to individuals in the social, behavioral, and health sciences in the United States, as well as to researchers on many continents around the globe.

FEATURES OF A CONCISE BOOK

This book contains several features to facilitate easy reading: The chapters are short; references and illustrations are kept to a minimum so as not to distract from the flow of the text; additional resources are listed at the end of each chapter; and a short glossary of key terms ends the book so that the reader can quickly grasp the nomenclature of this methodology. Many of the ideas presented in this book draw on my current research methods books (some coauthored by Plano Clark) from SAGE Publications and Pearson.

CHAPTERS IN THE BOOK

I begin with a definition of mixed methods and a description of key features of this methodology in Chapter 1. Chapter 2 identifies several steps that I use when students and faculty appear in my office wanting to design a mixed methods project. Unquestionably, to conduct a mixed methods study requires skill in both quantitative and qualitative research as well as mixed methods research, and in Chapter 3 I review the essential skills needed for this form of inquiry. I then turn in Chapter 4 to the centerpiece of all mixed methods projects—the design—and discuss the six major designs being used in projects today. Chapter 5 follows up on this discussion by focusing on how to draw a diagram of procedures for each type of design. With a design in mind, an individual planning a mixed methods project can consult Chapter 6, which discusses how to write the front end of the project: the introduction, including the purpose statement or study aims and the research questions. Two key issues in planning a project—sampling and integration—are discussed in Chapter 7 as they arise in the different types of mixed methods designs. Chapter 8 fast-forwards to the end of the process, after the study has been completed, and advances suggestions for publishing mixed methods research. Chapter 9 acknowledges the importance of maintaining high quality throughout a mixed methods project and reviews criteria being developed to assess the quality of a study. In Chapter 10, I summarize some of the scientific developments in mixed methods research that I have highlighted throughout the chapters in this book, and I look to the future by positioning mixed methods within the digital age of conducting research. In all chapters, I alternate the use of quantitative and qualitative research so as to equally emphasize these two approaches.

ACKNOWLEDGMENTS

I acknowledge the support of all of the participants in my mixed methods workshops across disciplines and across countries over the last 15 years. Thanks for your helpful comments. Also, I would like to thank my SAGE family that has supported my writing in research methods. Vicki Knight, publisher of research methods, statistics, and evaluation, has championed my work, and I appreciate the talent she brings to my projects. I would also like to acknowledge Tim Guetterman, my doctoral advisee and senior research assistant at the University of Nebraska–Lincoln, who has provided invaluable aid in all phases of this project and has brought insight and research skills to this book.

ABOUT THE AUTHOR

 **John W. Creswell** is a professor of educational psychology at the University of Nebraska–Lincoln. In addition to teaching at the University, he has authored numerous articles on mixed methods research, qualitative methodology, and general research design, as well as 22 books (including new editions), many of which focus on types of research designs, comparisons of different qualitative methodologies, and the nature and use of mixed methods research. His books have been translated into many languages and are used around the world. Dr. Creswell held the Clifton Institute Endowed Professor Chair for five years at the University of Nebraska–Lincoln. For an additional five years, he served as director at the Office of Qualitative and Mixed Methods Research at the University of Nebraska–Lincoln, which provided support for scholars incorporating qualitative and mixed methods research into projects for extramural funding. He served as founding coeditor for the *Journal of Mixed Methods Research* (SAGE) and has held the position of adjunct professor of family medicine at the University of Michigan, where he assisted investigators in the health sciences and education with research methodology for National Institutes of Health and National Science Foundation projects. He also served extensively as a consultant in the health services research area for the Veterans Health Administration. Dr. Creswell was a Senior Fulbright Scholar to South Africa and in 2008 lectured to faculty and students at five universities on mixed methods research in education and the health sciences. In 2012, he again was a Senior Fulbright Scholar, this time to Thailand. In 2011, he served as co-leader of a national working group at NIH developing "best practices" for mixed methods research in the health sciences. In the spring of 2013, Dr. Creswell was a visiting professor at Harvard's School of Public Health. In the summer of 2013, he conducted mixed methods training at Cambridge University in the UK. In 2014, he will be awarded an honorary doctorate from the University of Pretoria in South Africa.

CHAPTER 1

BASIC FEATURES OF MIXED METHODS RESEARCH

UNDERSTANDING MIXED ❖
METHODS RESEARCH

The best way to begin, I believe, is to reach an understanding of the basic characteristics of mixed methods research. As a field of **methodology** about 25 years old, this approach has common elements that can easily be identified. That is not to say that there is no disagreement about the core meaning of this approach. It can be viewed from a philosophical stance, in which epistemology and other philosophical assumptions take center stage. It can also be presented as a methodology, that is, as a research process originating from a broad philosophy and extending to interpretation and dissemination. Or it can be positioned within a transformative perspective, such as feminism or disability theory. Since these are all possibilities, it is crucial to recognize that several definitions exist depending on the perspective of the author.

My stance is to look at mixed methods as a **method**. This means that I will give it a distinct methods orientation, one in which data collection, analysis, and interpretation hold center stage. This is not to minimize the importance of philosophy or of methodology or of the research questions. It is simply to place emphasis on the methods, because they provide a specific, concrete way to enter the field of mixed methods.

❖ WHAT MIXED METHODS IS

Given this perspective, I see **mixed methods research** as:

> An approach to research in the social, behavioral, and health sciences in which the investigator gathers both quantitative (closed-ended) and qualitative (open-ended) data, integrates the two, and then draws interpretations based on the combined strengths of both sets of data to understand research problems.

A core assumption of this approach is that when an investigator combines statistical trends (**quantitative data**) with stories and personal experiences (**qualitative data**), this collective strength provides a better understanding of the research problem than either form of data alone.

❖ WHAT MIXED METHODS IS NOT

Given this definition, we can extrapolate several things that mixed methods is not:

1. Mixed methods is not simply the gathering of both quantitative and qualitative data. Although this form of research is helpful, it does not speak to the integration of the two data sources and play upon the strength that this combination brings to a study.

2. Mixed methods research is not simply a matter of using that label in your study. There are specific scientific techniques associated with this methodology, and reviewers familiar with mixed methods will be looking for them.

3. Mixed methods should not be confused with a mixed model approach to quantitative research, in which investigators conduct statistical analysis of fixed and random effects in a database.

4. Mixed methods is not simply an evaluation technique, such as formative plus summative evaluation, even though a researcher could collect and integrate both quantitative and qualitative data in performing such evaluation.

5. Mixed methods is not simply the addition of qualitative data to a quantitative design. Mixed methods can be employed in this way, but we can also add quantitative data to qualitative, and we need a rationale for doing it either way.

6. Mixed methods further is not simply the collection of multiple forms of qualitative data (e.g., interviews and observations), nor the collection of multiple types of quantitative data (e.g., survey data, experimental data). It involves the collection, analysis, and integration of *both* quantitative and qualitative data. In this way, the value of the different approaches to research (e.g., the trends as well as the stories and personal experiences) can contribute more to understanding a research problem than one form of data collection (quantitative or qualitative) could on its own. When multiple forms of qualitative data (or multiple forms of quantitative data) are collected, the term is *multimethod* research, not mixed methods research.

CORE CHARACTERISTICS ❖
OF MIXED METHODS

- Collection and analysis of quantitative and qualitative data in response to research questions
- Use of rigorous qualitative and quantitative methods
- Combination or integration of quantitative and qualitative data using a specific type of mixed methods design, and interpretation of this integration
- Sometimes, framing of the design within a philosophy or theory

In the remainder of this chapter, I will address each key feature in greater detail.

Collecting Quantitative and Qualitative Data

I start with the assumption that the two types of data differ and that they take different but equally important roles. A researcher using quantitative methods decides what to study, poses specific questions or hypotheses, measures variables to facilitate the finding of answers, uses statistical analysis to obtain information in order to answer the questions/hypotheses, and makes an interpretation of the results. This form of research is quite different from qualitative research, in which the investigator poses general questions and collects data in the form of text, audio recordings, or video recordings. A hallmark of qualitative research is that the researcher collects data by observing participants or directly asking them open-ended questions using tools such as interviews, focus group protocols, or questionnaires. After collecting qualitative data, the researcher conducts a thematic analysis and presents the findings in literary form, such as a story or narrative. Thus, both approaches follow the general process of research: Identify a problem, determine research questions, collect data, analyze data, and interpret results. However, the means of carrying out each of these stages differs considerably between the two methods.

Elements of both quantitative and qualitative research are included in a mixed methods study. It becomes important, then, to realize that a mixed methods researcher needs to be skilled in both quantitative and qualitative approaches. Furthermore, to make the most of a mixed methods design, investigators need to understand the advantages and the disadvantages that accrue from both quantitative and qualitative research. See Table 1.1 for a brief comparison of quantitative and qualitative research.

Using Rigorous Methods

Although both quantitative and qualitative research flow into a mixed methods study, this does not mean that the scope of each approach will be reduced. Over the years, several authors have advanced criteria for what constitutes rigorous research from either a quantitative or qualitative perspective. We need to pay attention to those guidelines, whether they are the CONSORT guidelines in the medical field or informal guidelines for qualitative research advanced in research design books such as *Research Design: Qualitative, Quantitative, and Mixed Methods Approaches* (Creswell, 2014). Key elements of rigor for both quantitative and qualitative methods are:

- Type of design (e.g., experiment, ethnography)
- Permissions for gaining access to the site

Table 1.1   Advantages and Limitations of Qualitative and Quantitative Research

Qualitative Research	
Advantages	**Disadvantages**
Provides detailed perspectives of a few people	Has limited generalizability
Captures the voices of participants	Provides only soft data (not hard data, such as numbers)
Allows participants' experiences to be understood in context	Studies few people
Is based on the views of participants, not of the researcher	Is highly subjective
Appeals to people's enjoyment of stories	Minimizes use of researcher's expertise due to reliance on participants
Quantitative Research	
Advantages	**Disadvantages**
Draws conclusions for large numbers of people	Is impersonal, dry
Analyzes data efficiently	Does not record the words of participants
Investigates relationships within data	Provides limited understanding of the context of participants
Examines probable causes and effects	Is largely researcher driven
Controls bias	
Appeals to people's preference for numbers	

- Sampling approach (systematic vs. purposeful)
- Number of participants
- Types of data to be collected (e.g., text, audio and video recordings, test score questionnaire responses)
- Instruments used to collect the data (e.g., surveys, observational checklists, open-ended interviews, focus group protocols)
- Organization and cleaning of the database as the first step in data analysis
- Later data analysis procedures, ranging from basic to more sophisticated approaches (e.g., descriptive to inferential, coding to theme development)
- Approaches to establish the validity and reliability of the data (e.g., internal validity vs. validation strategies)

Integrating Data

No topic in the field of mixed methods research is so confusing as the question of how to integrate the datasets. How do you reconcile words or text data with numbers or numeric data? Researchers are often simply not familiar with these procedures because they typically deal with only one type of data (i.e., quantitative or qualitative).

To understand where and how to integrate the databases requires first knowing something about the types of **mixed methods designs** (these designs will be briefly introduced here and developed in more depth in Chapter 4). There are three basic designs at the center of all mixed methods projects, as well as three advanced designs that constitute add-ons to the basic designs.

The three basic mixed methods designs are:

- A *convergent design*, in which the intent of the research is to collect both quantitative and qualitative data, analyze both datasets, and then *merge* the results of the two sets of data analyses with the purpose of comparing the results (some say validating one set of results with the other).
- An *explanatory sequential design*, in which the intent is to first use quantitative methods and then use qualitative methods to help *explain* the quantitative results in more depth. This is an easy, straightforward design.
- An *exploratory sequential design*, in which the intent is first to explore a problem with qualitative methods because the questions may not be known, the population may be understudied or little understood, or the site may be difficult to access. After this initial exploration, the researcher uses the qualitative findings to *build* a second quantitative phase of the project. This phase may involve designing an instrument to measure variables in the study, developing activities for an experimental intervention, or designing a typology that is then measured using existing instruments. In the third phase, the quantitative instrument, intervention, or variables are used in a quantitative data collection and analysis procedure.

One of these basic designs is typically found in every mixed methods study, either explicitly or implicitly. In some studies, additional features are added to the basic design. I call the resulting design an *advanced design*. Here are examples of advanced designs popular in the mixed methods literature today:

- *Intervention designs* are those in which the researchers employ a convergent design, an explanatory design, or an exploratory design within a larger experimental framework. Simply put, the investigator gathers qualitative data at some phase during the experiment, such as before the trial, during the trial, or after the trial. Integration in this case consists of *embedding* the qualitative data within an experimental trial.
- *Social justice* or *transformative designs* are those in which the researcher includes a social justice framework that surrounds the convergent, explanatory, or exploratory design. This framework flows into the mixed methods study at different points, but it becomes a constant focus of the study aimed at improving the lives of individuals in our society today (e.g., a feminist social justice design). Integration in this type of design involves *threading* the social justice concept throughout the study.
- *Multistage evaluation designs* are longitudinal studies consisting of many stages conducted over time with the central objective of a sustained line of inquiry. Within this objective would be the use of multiple mixed methods studies (as well as separate quantitative and qualitative studies) using convergent, explanatory, or exploratory designs. A prime example of this design would be the evaluation over time of the design, piloting, and implementation of a program in a community. Many stages of research would be involved in this program evaluation study: a needs assessment, a conceptual framework, the testing of the program, and a follow-up to the program. In this case, integration consists of *expanding* one stage into other stages over time.

Integration can then take several forms: merging, explaining, building, and embedding, depending on the type of design. It is common for the designs to emerge in a project rather than being preplanned. In addition, variations on these basic and advanced designs are allowed and often used. Still, it is important for learners of mixed methods research to understand the six designs (three basic and three advanced), because these designs will be the popular types found in the literature.

Using a Framework

The advanced designs suggest the importance of various conceptual and theoretical frameworks that are often used in mixed methods research. We see in many mixed methods studies the use of a social or behavioral science framework that surrounds the mixed methods study. For example, a researcher may use a leadership theory to advance an explanatory sequential design and to present both the quantitative and qualitative results. Alternatively, a behavioral change model may surround a mixed methods study in the health sciences. As suggested by the social justice design, the framework may be a transformative or advocacy framework that surrounds the project in order to advance the needs of a marginalized group (e.g., a mixed methods study of racial profiling). These theoretical frameworks fall under either *social or behavioral theoretical models* or *transformative theoretical models.*

Another framework that may be used in a mixed methods study is a philosophical perspective. Philosophical frameworks are general beliefs and assumptions about research, such as how researchers discover knowledge. We all bring our understanding of the nature of the world and our assumptions about what information needs to be collected (e.g., subjective knowledge versus objective knowledge) to our study of a research problem. Research fields differ in terms of the importance of making these philosophical assumptions explicit or implicit in a study. Regardless of your field, it is important to acknowledge that our values and beliefs shape our orientation to research, how we gather data, the biases we bring to research, and whether we see our investigations as more emerging or fixed.

❖ RECOMMENDATIONS FROM THIS CHAPTER

I would recommend that researchers planning or conducting a mixed methods study be able to:

- define mixed methods research;
- recognize whether their proposed study meets this definition; and
- evaluate their idea for a mixed methods project by asking themselves the following questions to determine whether it contains the four key characteristics of a mixed method study:
  - o Am I collecting and analyzing quantitative and qualitative data in response to research questions?
  - o Am I using rigorous qualitative and quantitative methods?

o Am I combining or integrating the quantitative and qualitative data, interpreting this integration, and using a mixed methods design?
o Am I framing the study within a philosophy and/or a theory?

ADDITIONAL READINGS ❖

Creswell, J. W., & Plano Clark, V. L. (2011). *Designing and conducting mixed methods research* (2nd ed.). Thousand Oaks, CA: SAGE.

Johnson, R. B., Onwuegbuzie, A. J., & Turner, L. A. (2007). Toward a definition of mixed methods research. *Journal of Mixed Methods Research, 1*(2), 112–133.

CHAPTER 2

STEPS IN DESIGNING A MIXED METHODS STUDY

❖ TOPICS IN THE CHAPTER

- An "office visit" to learn mixed methods design
- Steps in designing a mixed methods study

❖ THE NEED FOR PLANNING A STUDY

Individuals wanting to conduct a mixed methods study often turn to books on the subject, consult faculty or resource persons who have conducted a mixed methods study, or attend workshops or conferences where they can learn about the methodology. Sometimes these resources are not available, especially to scholars new to mixed methods or to individuals around the globe in far-off countries. This chapter addresses the steps that I typically take when advising researchers about how to conduct a mixed methods study. It will be as if you have walked into my office and I am helping you, step by step, to design your mixed methods project. Unquestionably, not all of these topics can be adequately covered in a single session, and our work together will take several meetings.

First, I will inquire whether you have an audience for your mixed methods study (e.g., graduate committee, journal, books, funding agency);

access to and permission to use both quantitative and qualitative data; skills in both qualitative and quantitative research (see Chapter 3); and an open mind about using multiple perspectives to examine a research problem. I will then suggest topics that we might discuss, not presented in the order typically followed in conducting a research project but offered in a way that will allow you to easily begin your project (e.g., starting with what you want to accomplish). I introduce this order intentionally, so that you can move forward in a concrete, simple way before tackling the harder elements of design. After concluding the planning process, however, we will reorganize the steps into the logical order typically found in planning a study. Not all steps in the mixed methods research process will be included in this discussion, but the major ones will be covered so that you have a solid foundation for your study.

STEPS IN THE PROCESS

The steps in the mixed methods process that I will discuss with you are:

1. Drafting a working title for the project

2. Identifying the problem or issue underlying the need for the study

3. Indicating the intent or general question to be answered

4. Specifying the types of data collection and analysis to be used

5. Identifying reasons for using mixed methods in your project

6. Considering the inclusion of a worldview discussion and a theory discussion

7. Defining mixed methods

8. Choosing a mixed methods design

9. Drawing a figure of your design

10. Considering methodological and validity issues in your study

11. Writing a mixed methods study aim or purpose

12. Adding research questions (quantitative, qualitative, and mixed) that match your design

❖ THE WORKING TITLE

Starting with the title may seem like a strange place to begin. However, I view the title as a major placeholder in a study—a focus, if you will, for the entire project. Taking a stand on a title is therefore an essential part of beginning to design a study. Granted, the title will change and shift over time as the project becomes more and more clearly defined and focused.

There are several key elements that must be included in a good mixed methods title:

- The topic being addressed (e.g., palliative care or bullying).
- The participants in the study (i.e., the individuals from whom the data are being collected, such as elderly patients or senior citizens) and perhaps the site where the participants reside (e.g., a major university or a senior center).
- The words *mixed methods* to denote the methodology being used.
- Neutral language (at least at the outset) that does not lean the study toward either a quantitative or a qualitative orientation. Stay away from words that convey a qualitative leaning, such as *explore, meaning*, or *discover*. Also stay away from words that convey a quantitative orientation, such as *relationship, correlation*, or *explanation*. The goal is to compose a "neutral" title, since mixed methods resides between quantitative and qualitative research.

In addition, keep the title short (say, under 10 words), and perhaps use a two-part title separated by a colon. Quantitative and qualitative research may be mentioned in the title. Here are a couple of good examples:

Example 1. Unwritten rules of talking to doctors about depression: Integrating quantitative and qualitative methods (Wittink, Barg, & Gallo, 2006)

Example 2. Students' persistence in a distributed doctoral program in educational leadership in higher education: A mixed methods study (Ivankova & Stick, 2007)

❖ THE PROBLEM UNDERLYING
THE NEED FOR THE STUDY

Next, it is important to write a short paragraph about the problem or issue that underlies the need for the study. This is not an easy paragraph to write, but it is one of the most important components of a good study. If a reader is looking at a journal article and does not find a compelling reason to continue reading (i.e., a problem), he or she will quickly lose interest in the article. Thus, you need to think like a novelist, who must grab the attention of his or her readers in the opening passages.

One reason why this paragraph is difficult to write lies in a basic understanding of the nature of research. Research is intended to address problems. This may be stating the obvious, but I am not always sure that researchers understand this important fact. Also, it is sometimes difficult to describe the problem because it may be easier to write about what is being done rather than what "needs" to be done. I find many problem statement passages oriented toward "what exists" instead of "what needs to be fixed." So, in having you write this paragraph for a mixed methods plan, I will ask you to think about the "problem" or issue that needs to be addressed. In some cases, more than one issue may lead to a need for a study. Also, I will ask you to consider stating more than that "there is a need in the literature" or a "gap" or that the literature has shown "mixed results." These are good rationales for a problem, but I also like to see what I would call "practical" problems—problems that reside in practice or in the real world that need to be addressed. What do policymakers, or health providers, or teachers need? Describe some combination of real-world problems and deficiencies in the literature.

THE INTENT OR ❖
QUESTION TO BE ANSWERED

After composing the title and identifying the problem, pose the general intent (or aim) of the study. This can be phrased in a single sentence. You will use it later in the purpose statement or study aim section of the plan. One way to get to this intent is to consider what you want to accomplish by the end of the study. What is the overriding aim of the project?

If you wrote this statement out during our hypothetical office visit, I would be curious to see how it was phrased. This phrasing would be a tip-off about the type of design that might be most suitable for you as well as an indication of your skill level. I would be looking for quantitative or qualitative words that exhibited your orientation and that would likely point to the type of mixed methods design that would be most appealing to you.

❖ THE TYPES OF DATA COLLECTION AND DATA ANALYSIS TO BE USED

Next, it is important to identify the types of quantitative as well as qualitative data collection and analysis that will be proposed. Draw two columns, and then list under each the forms of data collection and analysis that will be used in your project. I typically coach researchers to identify the following items (for both quantitative and qualitative data) under data collection:

- Participants
- Site for the research
- Number of participants
- Types of information to be collected (e.g., measures and variables quantitatively, central phenomena qualitatively)
- Types of data (e.g., instrument, records, interviews)

I also have them list the specific forms of data analysis they anticipate using:

- Procedures for organizing the data (e.g., putting it into an SPSS file, having the audio recording transcribed)
- Basic data analysis procedures (e.g., coding qualitative data, descriptive analysis of quantitative data)
- More advanced data analysis procedures (e.g., comparing groups or relating variables quantitatively, developing themes or a chronology qualitatively)
- Software programs that might be used (e.g., SPSS, MAXQDA)

❖ REASONS FOR USING MIXED METHODS

The next step in the process is to write a paragraph identifying the reasons for using mixed methods as a methodology. I believe that we need to advance a **rationale for mixed methods** today, much like the rationale for qualitative research typically needed for federal proposals. Perhaps, as the methodology becomes more widely known and accepted, a rationale for its use will not be needed in the future. In the meantime, we need to convince readers that mixed methods is the appropriate methodology to use in our mixed methods studies. How is this done?

I see a two-part answer to this question. First, there is a general rationale for using mixed methods in a study. It is appropriate to use mixed methods when the use of quantitative research or qualitative research alone is insufficient for gaining an understanding of the problem. Using only one method may be insufficient because of the inherent weaknesses of each approach. Quantitative research does not adequately investigate personal stories and meanings or deeply probe the perspectives of individuals. Qualitative research does not enable us to generalize from a small group of people to a large population. It does not precisely measure what people in general feel. In short, all research methods have both strengths and weaknesses, and the combination of the strengths of both provides a good rationale for using mixed methods (quantitative research provides an opportunity for generalization and precision; qualitative research offers an in-depth experience of individual perspectives). Alternatively, we might consider how the strengths of one form of research make up for the weaknesses of the other. This was the core argument advanced for the use of mixed methods in early writings about this methodology (see Rossman & Wilson, 1985).

At a more specific level, the combination of quantitative and qualitative research enables us to:

- obtain two different perspectives, one drawn from closed-ended response data (quantitative) and one drawn from open-ended personal data (qualitative);
- obtain a more comprehensive view and more data about the problem than either the quantitative or the qualitative perspective;
- add to instrument data (quantitative information) details about the setting, place, and context of personal experiences (qualitative information);
- conduct preliminary exploration with individuals (qualitative research) to make sure that instruments, measures, and intervention (quantitative research) actually fit the participants and site being studied; and
- add qualitative data to our experimental trials (quantitative research) by, for example, identifying participants to recruit and interventions to use, assessing the personal experiences of participants during the trial, and carrying out follow-up to further explain the outcomes.

If you are planning a mixed methods study, I recommend that you identify both the general rationale for using mixed methods and the specific rationales by looking over the above list and determining if any of them fit your particular study. These specific rationales are linked to specific types of mixed methods designs (as discussed later in Chapter 4).

❖ SPECIFYING A WORLDVIEW OR THEORY

We all bring a worldview (or paradigm) to our research, whether we make it explicit or not. This worldview is a set of beliefs or values that inform how we undertake a study (Guba, 1990). With this topic, we have entered the realm of the philosophy of conducting research. These beliefs may relate to what types of evidence we use to make claims (**epistemology**) or whether we feel that reality is multiple or singular (**ontology**). For example, we may feel that reality is found in a theory that helps to explain behavior among a large number of people or that reality is better determined by different individual perspectives than one general explanation. In terms of how we proceed with our research, we may approach it more as an emerging design with changes shaping our next steps or as a fixed design where we do not dare change a hypothesis or build in additional data beyond what we initially decide to measure. This idea speaks to the methodological assumptions we make about our research.

Where do these beliefs that we hold come from? I think that we are socialized as researchers to hold certain beliefs. Within a field or discipline, there are typical problems pursued, distinct ways to study these problems, and approaches to disseminating our scholarly work. Thus, a belief or value regarding research starts when we are socialized as students, and then as faculty and scholars within a community of researchers. This was the rationale for beliefs in paradigms first announced years ago by Thomas Kuhn in his book *The Structure of Scientific Revolutions* (1962).

Mixed methods writers from the earliest days were concerned about what philosophical tenets provided a foundation for this method of inquiry. People often associated methods with philosophy, and when researchers, for example, collected qualitative focus group data, it was often associated with more of a constructivist worldview of understanding multiple meanings. When researchers gathered data on instruments, it reflected a reductionistic perspective associated with postpositivism (Creswell, 2013). How can two different worldviews coexist, as is being suggested in mixed methods?

The answer mixed methods researchers have given to this question is to look for one underlying philosophy that informs both quantitative and qualitative data collection. Thus, some mixed methods writers adhere to **pragmatism** (i.e., "what works" and practice) as a philosophy, others to critical realism, and still others to dialectic pluralism. The choice depends on how much a researcher knows about these different philosophies and which one seems to resonate with a particular mixed methods project.

A companion issue is whether to be explicit about worldview in the design of a mixed methods study. In the health sciences, we do not see much philosophy explicitly stated; in the social and behavioral sciences, it is common to encounter it. When it is inserted in a mixed methods plan, the responsibility falls to the researcher to explain it and provide ample references so that readers can follow up on it. Further, the researcher needs to be explicit about how it informs the mixed methods project.

Theories, in contrast to philosophical assumptions, are commonly used in mixed methods studies. Researchers need to plan for determining what theory to use and how it will specifically be incorporated into the mixed methods project. A theory in quantitative research is an explanation as to what the researcher expects to find. This theory can be used to explain, predict, and generalize, and it informs the research questions and hypotheses in a study. A theory in qualitative research can also be an explanation; it can also be a lens that informs the phases of the research process.

In social, behavioral, and health science research, the theory may be one drawn from social science, such as a theory of diffusion, leadership, or behavioral change. One finds these theories in the literature and locates them by closely reading journal articles and research studies that include theories. They typically inform the quantitative side of research, and help in determining what questions to ask. In qualitative research, they may be advanced at the beginning of a study (e.g., an ethnographic theory of acculturation), or they may emerge through data collection (e.g., in grounded theory research). It is helpful in mixed methods studies to make these theories explicit, to describe them in some detail, to identify the author(s) of the theory, and to suggest how the theory informs a particular phase in the mixed methods study (e.g., the quantitative component of data collection).

Another type of theory would be a transformative, participatory, or advocacy theory. For example, in mixed methods studies, we find that a theoretical lens may be drawn from feminist theories, social economic theories, disability theories, or racial or ethnic theories. These theoretical orientations have become important lenses informing many different phases of a mixed methods project. A popular theory (or perspective) in the health sciences has been community-based participatory research (CBPR), in which stakeholders or community members become active participants in many phases of the research—helping to determine the problem, assisting in the design of the research questions, collaborating in data collection and analysis, and serving to disseminate the results. It is hard to find a mixed methods study today that is not informed by a social science or participatory type of theory.

❖ DEFINING MIXED METHODS

Now your design of a mixed methods study is beginning to drill down into some specific areas. One of these is the definition of mixed methods research. At the beginning of a methods discussion in a journal article or proposal, the authors define their methodology (e.g., randomized controlled trial, quasi-experiment, ethnography). Since mixed methods is the methodology of choice, a definition of the mixed methods plan is needed.

This definition needs to state that mixed methods (see the core characteristics in Chapter 1):

- is a research methodology for conducting a study in the social, behavioral, and health sciences;
- involves collection and analysis of both quantitative and qualitative data in response to research questions;
- integrates the two sources of data by combining or merging them, connecting them (e.g., qualitative follows quantitative), or embedding them (e.g., qualitative data flows into an experimental trial); and
- incorporates these procedures into a design or plan for conducting the study, where the study is often framed by philosophical assumptions or theories.

❖ DIAGRAMS, PROCEDURES, AND CHOICE OF DESIGN

Your design may change over the course of a study, but it is helpful to identify a design you might use and then draw a diagram of this design to share with others (e.g., committee members, audiences at conferences, reviewers of proposals).

It is important at this stage to first consider a basic design (recall that the basic designs are the convergent design, the explanatory sequential design, and the exploratory sequential design, to be discussed in more detail in Chapter 4). A helpful resource is *Designing and Conducting Mixed Methods Research* (Creswell & Plano Clark, 2011), which illustrates the types of diagrams that could be drawn for each design.

During our office visit, I would ask you to draw a picture of your basic design and talk about the intent of using the design. I would review some of the basic notation used to talk about research designs. You might state this intent quite simply:

Example 1. For an Explanatory Sequential Design

Quantitative leads to qualitative for the purpose of explaining the quantitative results

Next, you need to draw out your basic design in a simple, uncompli-cated diagram. Later you can add in features such as specific "procedures" or "products" that you hope to realize at each step. I would also have you list the steps in conducting the design (see Chapter 5). Once you have drawn this basic design, consider whether you want to add a major feature into your study, such as an experiment (or intervention trial), a theoretical framework that informs all phases of your project, or an evaluation perspec-tive. These additions need to be drawn into your diagram, and they will result in an advanced design. Finally, I would talk about how you can add features into your diagram of the design, such as a timeline, an appropriate title, notation, or other features discussed later in Chapter 5.

POTENTIAL METHODOLOGICAL ❖ CHALLENGES AND THREATS TO VALIDITY

Just as those who conduct qualitative and quantitative research need to address factors that would compromise the validity of their studies, mixed methods researchers need to consider threats to validity specific to con-ducting a mixed methods study. At this point, consider these threats based on the design you chose (Creswell, in press) (the designs are detailed in Chapter 4). If you are using a convergent design, consider whether the quali-tative central phenomena and quantitative variables or constructs are parallel. Other threats in this design may arise depending on whether you decide to use equal or unequal sample sizes for the qualitative and quantitative data, whether they have parallel units of analysis (i.e., individual or groups), how you merge the results of the two analyses, and how you explain divergent results. The potential for other threats arises with the explana-tory sequential design. In this case, I would encourage you to think about the following decisions: what quantitative results need follow-up, how you will select the sample of follow-up participants, how you will develop relevant interview questions, and how you will ensure that the qualitative data indeed explain the quantitative results. Finally, if you are using an exploratory sequential design, I would focus on the issues that arise when building from the qualitative to the quantitative phase. When developing an instrument, for example, you need to translate the qualitative findings into items or scales and then use good psychometric procedures, such as examining the reliability and validity evidence. Noting these threats is an important part of planning your study.

❖ A MIXED METHODS STUDY AIM OR PURPOSE

Next, you need to develop a study aim, that is, a paragraph that establishes the purpose of your study. This paragraph should include what you intend to accomplish during the study, the type of design you will use and a brief definition of it, the methods of quantitative and qualitative data collection and analysis you will use, and your rationale for using mixed methods. This study aim or purpose needs to be crafted to reflect the type of design being used in your study (see Chapter 6).

❖ QUANTITATIVE, QUALITATIVE, AND MIXED METHODS QUESTIONS

With your study aim in hand, it is time to craft your research questions. You will create three types of questions: quantitative questions or hypotheses, qualitative questions, and mixed methods questions. This will require going over some of the basics of writing each type of question (see Chapter 6). In particular, this step will require learning how to write a mixed methods question, and to state it in such a way that it reflects the outcome expected in using a mixed methods design.

❖ REORGANIZING THE STEPS

The final step in conducting a study is to organize the components into the logical order typically found in a good research plan or proposal. These components, in order, are:

1. The draft title

2. The problem leading to a need for the study

3. The worldview and/or the theory used in the study

4. The purpose or study aim

5. The research questions

6. The rationale for using mixed methods research

7. A definition for mixed methods research

8. The types of quantitative and qualitative data to be collected and analyzed

9. The mixed methods design to be used and a diagram of the procedures

RECOMMENDATIONS FROM THIS CHAPTER ❖

In this chapter I have taken you through the steps that I typically use to advise individuals planning a mixed methods study. I do believe in preplanning a study rather than allowing it entirely to evolve. I also believe that the steps originally planned can be revised during the completion of a project and that the steps conveyed here are not a definitive, unchanging guide. I began with easy steps—the title, the problem, the central intent, and the data collection—rather than with more abstract ideas such as the philosophy or theory. I included the reasons for using mixed methods and gave you a definition. I then had you focus on the type of design you would use and draft a diagram of your procedures. Finally, with this information in place, I asked you to write out the study aim or purpose and the specific quantitative, qualitative, and mixed methods research questions. The steps can then be reorganized to present the logic often seen in a research process, and you can add in additional elements not described in these steps (e.g., ethical issues, the practical significance of the study, potential limitations). The steps outlined here, however, will provide a good starting point for designing a rigorous, sophisticated mixed methods study.

ADDITIONAL READINGS ❖

Creswell, J. W. (in press). Revisiting mixed methods and advancing scientific practices. In S. N. Hesse-Biber & R. B. Johnson (Eds.), *Oxford handbook of mixed and multiple research methods*. Oxford, UK: Oxford University Press.

Creswell, J. W., Fetters, M. D., Plano Clark, V. L., & Morales, A. (2009). Mixed methods intervention trials. In S. Andrew & E. J. Halcomb (Eds.), *Mixed methods research for nursing and the health sciences* (pp. 161–180). Oxford, UK: Wiley.

Creswell, J. W., & Zhang, W. (2009). The application of mixed methods designs to trauma research. *Journal of Traumatic Stress, 22,* 612–621. doi: 10.1002/jts.20479

Ivankova, N. V., & Stick, S. L. (2007). Students' persistence in a distributed doctoral program in educational leadership in higher education: A mixed methods study. *Research in Higher Education, 48,* 93–135. doi: 10.1007/s11162-006-9025-4

Kuhn, T. S. (1962). *The structure of scientific revolutions.* Chicago, IL: University of Chicago Press.

Wittink, M. N., Barg, F. K., & Gallo, J. J. (2006). Unwritten rules of talking to doctors about depression: Integrating qualitative and quantitative methods. *Annals of Family Medicine, 4,* 302–309. doi: 10.1370/afm.558

CHAPTER 3

SKILLS NEEDED TO CONDUCT MIXED METHODS RESEARCH

REQUIREMENTS FOR ❖ CONDUCTING MIXED METHODS

When I introduced the core characteristics of mixed methods research, I included the component of using rigorous quantitative and qualitative methods. To conduct these methods requires skill training and recognition of what constitutes "rigor." In this chapter I talk about the skills needed by a mixed methods researcher and the specific rigorous methods in both quantitative and qualitative research needed for a mixed methods study. For those unfamiliar with either form of research, this chapter presents a short course in these methods in simple terms.

Individuals who engage in mixed methods research sometimes feel that because both forms of data are gathered and analyzed, they need to abbreviate either the quantitative or qualitative component or both in a mixed methods study. However, good mixed methods studies consist of rigorous procedures for both components. This means that the researcher is required to know the skills of both quantitative and qualitative research, or at least the methods associated with each.

Alternatively, a researcher could belong to an academic team of individuals having diverse methodological skills. One physician said to me in a workshop, "What is the minimum I need to know to conduct mixed methods research?" I answered that either you need to know about data collection and data analysis for both quantitative and qualitative research, or you need to join a team with individuals who have skills in this area. Another question that I often hear is, "What level of education is needed for an individual to engage in mixed methods research?" This is another good question. The collection and analysis of *both* quantitative and qualitative research requires not only a sophisticated knowledge of research but also a skill set that will enable one to conduct this form of inquiry. It is suitable for individuals with doctoral degrees, which may rule out people with a master's or undergraduate students. At least, for a while I thought this was the case, but when I judged a competition for the best undergraduate research at a South African university, three of the five finalists had what I would call a mixed methods orientation to their research. In these three projects, the undergraduates were gathering and analyzing both quantitative and qualitative research. What seemed to be lacking, however, was full integration of the two databases, an approach consistent with a sophisticated mixed methods project.

> Mixed methods requires the researcher to acquire skills in both quantitative and qualitative research.

When asked about the skill set needed to undertake a mixed methods study, I often refer to the general procedure being used in my graduate program at the University of Nebraska–Lincoln. Graduate students enter my mixed methods course after they have completed classes on statistics and quantitative designs (e.g., experimental designs) and one or two qualitative research classes. I say that moving ahead in mixed methods requires skills in both quantitative and qualitative research.

MIXED METHODS TEAMS ❖

Unfortunately, most individuals do not have the luxury of building a comprehensive skill set. They find themselves on research teams undertaking a mixed methods study. In fact, there is a growing presence of mixed methods teams in academia because of the increased presence of interdisciplinary research. These teams often consist of individuals with different methodological orientations—quantitative versus qualitative skills. Team members who have skills in mixed methods may be a bridge between these two groups and facilitate the conversation about differences in thinking when they appear. We might have a medical sociologist sitting next to a biostatistician, or an anthropologist working on a team with a measurement specialist. In global research settings, the diversity of participants on a team may be even more pronounced, with individuals bringing their own local cultural norms to the research table.

Then there is the question of how team members interact. When academic teams work on a problem, they may relate from their own multidisciplinary perspective (working parallel to their own discipline) or from an interdisciplinary perspective (working across disciplinary fields) (see O'Cathain, Murphy, & Nicholl, 2008a). Overlaying these methodological differences may be the extent to which individuals cross disciplinary boundaries or stay within their own field's perspective as they work on a team. O'Cathain et al. (2008a, p. 1579) advanced possible configurations as shown in Table 3.1.

In current writings, we see that successful mixed methods teams have research support, have members with a range of expertise, engage in either multidisciplinary or interdisciplinary interactions, hold respect for diverse methodological orientations, and have a good leader who bridges across the areas of expertise and methodological persuasions. This leader pays attention to team composition, gives equal treatment to diverse methodologies, helps to shape dialogue, and values and involves all team members in decisions (Brannen & Moss, 2012). This leader also constructs a shared vision and develops a history of working together. Moreover, the team leader for a mixed methods project ideally has experience in quantitative, qualitative, and mixed methods research.

Table 3.1 Different Disciplinary Configurations of Members on a Mixed Methods Team

Team A: Principal investigator (medical) led the quantitative component; sociologist led the qualitative component and was responsible for parts of the quantitative component; statistician; and project researchers
Team B: Principal investigator (social scientist) led the qualitative and quantitative components; clinicians; psychologist; statistician; and two project researchers
Team C: Principal investigator (clinical) led the qualitative and quantitative components with two project researchers

Source: O'Cathain, Murphy, & Nicholl (2008, p. 1579). Permission granted by SAGE Publications.

❖ INDIVIDUAL SKILLS IN RESEARCH

For individuals engaging in mixed methods research, a general understanding of the flow of activities in the research design process is essential. This process holds true whether the study is quantitative, qualitative, or mixed methods. The process can be easily described this way:

- Identify a *research problem* or issue that needs to be addressed.
- *Review the literature* about the problem to establish a need for the study. Part of this literature may frame the study within a theoretical orientation.
- Indicate the *purpose* or aim of the study and the major objective to be accomplished, and narrow this purpose or aim to specific research questions (or hypotheses) that will be answered during the progress of the research.
- Select a *research design* or a plan for procedures for conducting the study.
- Collect data to answer the research questions by using rigorous procedures to gather information.
- Analyze the data collected to assess how the research questions were answered.
- Interpret the findings in light of existing literature and theories.
- Disseminate the study to different audiences.
- Keep ethical issues in mind in all phases of the research, especially from data collection through dissemination of the findings.

This is a process that I have followed in writing all of my books about research methods. It holds for both quantitative and qualitative research, but with differences between the two approaches residing not in the general process structure as indicated above, but in how each part of the process unfolds in an actual research study.

SKILLS IN QUANTITATIVE RESEARCH ❖

It might be helpful, then, to review how this process unfolds first in quantitative research and then in qualitative research. Quantitative research is a research approach in which investigators:

- Identify a theory that guides the development of research questions and hypotheses.
- Frame these questions and hypotheses in terms of variables or constructs and array them in terms of independent, covariate, mediating, and dependent variables to specify their relationships.
- Select a research design for the procedures of the study based on accepted designs, such as experiments (and their variations), surveys, single subject designs, or correlational studies (see Creswell, 2012). The design could also be one typically used in the health sciences, such as an observational or explanatory study (e.g., descriptive or case series, cohort study, case-control study, retrospective historical cohort study, cross-sectional study), or an experimental design that evaluates the effect of an intervention on study subjects (e.g., meta-analysis, randomized controlled trial, systematic review, trial with self-controls, cross-over study, nonrandomized trial).
- Gather numeric data on closed-ended scales, such as instruments or behavioral checklists, or from existent reports and documents, such as school attendance reports or patient audit histories.
- Statistically analyze the numeric data by using procedures that yield tables or graphs reporting results such as descriptive analyses, inferential analyses, effect sizes, and confidence intervals. Use statistical software programs to help analyze the data.
- Report the research in a reasonably standardized format that is consistent from one report to another and includes an introduction, an overview of the literature, a description of the methods, a description of the results, and the discussion.

- Ensure that your report is of high quality by including topics such as generalizability, bias, validity, reliability, and replicability.

This is, of course, only a general picture of the steps involved in conducting a quantitative study. There are more specific guidelines; for example, an experimental intervention trial might follow the CONSORT 2010 statement in the *Annals of Internal Medicine* (Schulz, Altman, & Moher, 2010). Further, I have drafted a checklist that I use for a complete methods discussion for a quantitative project (recall that mixed methods research focuses in on the methods of a study). It is shown in Table 3.2.

Table 3.2 Checklist for a Rigorous Quantitative Methods Discussion

General:

____ Provide a rationale for why quantitative research is well suited for studying the research problem (e.g., interest in factors that influence outcomes, a comparison of groups, testing a theory).

____ Describe the type of quantitative research design that will be used (e.g., experimental, quasi-experimental, single subject, correlational, survey).

____ Explain why the design is well suited to address the problem.

____ State particular validity threats associated with the use of the design.

Quantitative Data Collection:

____ Identify the research site for the study.

____ Identify permissions that have been granted (including institutional review board permission).

____ Indicate how participants will be recruited to the study.

____ Identify the number of participants in the study.

____ Indicate the different types of data that will be collected (e.g., instrumental data, observational data, numeric public data).

____ Identify additional information about each data type (e.g., reliability and validity scores for instruments used, reliability strategies for use with observational data, reliability of public information, use of standard procedures, training for data collectors).

Quantitative Data Analysis:

____ Mention data input procedures for compiling a quantitative database.

____ Review procedures that will be used to clean the database.

____ State the quantitative software data analysis program that will be used.

____ Indicate the types of analyses that will be conducted to check for response statistics (e.g., return rate, response bias).

____ Identify the types of descriptive analysis that will be carried out to address descriptive research questions/hypotheses.

____ Identify the types of inferential analysis that will be conducted to address relationship and comparison questions/hypotheses.

____ Identify the procedures that will be used to check for effect size and confidence intervals.

____ Discuss the types of tables that will be presented to convey statistical results.

This checklist provides guidance for those developing a rigorous quantitative section for their mixed methods projects. It focuses on the components of data collection and analysis, and it augments texts on quantitative methods that describe the procedures typically used.

SKILLS IN QUALITATIVE RESEARCH ❖

Qualitative research proceeds through the processes of research identified above, but at many parts of the research its procedures differ from those of quantitative research. I will relate this discussion to the topics that I used to describe a quantitative study so that you can make an easy comparison between the two forms of research. In qualitative research:

- The inquirer may start with a theory that guides the research questions, but this theory is modified during the research rather than being fixed. The key idea is to let the research evolve and change based on what the investigator learns from the participants in the study.
- To best learn from participants, the researcher poses general, open-ended questions, allowing the individuals in the study to provide

information without constraints. The use of variables or constructs would limit the study, and therefore independent, dependent, mediating, and other kinds of variables are not stated in qualitative research. Instead, the inquirer identifies a key topic—called a *central phenomenon*—and explores it with open-ended questions to participants. For example, a central phenomenon might be "remaining silent," and the researcher might explore what this term means for participants in a business organization.

- The types of designs used in qualitative research differ from the designs used in quantitative research. Rather than emerging out of an experimental orientation, qualitative designs came from fields such as sociology, psychology, and the humanities. They are not called *experiments* or *surveys*, but their names reflect how the research might proceed. For example, in narrative qualitative designs, we learn about the stories of individual lives. In phenomenological qualitative designs, we explore how different people experience the same construct, such as loneliness. In grounded theory, we generate a theory based on the views of participants, not from an off-the-shelf theory that has been developed from a different sample at a different location. In case study qualitative research, we explore a single or multiple cases to learn about how people address a specific issue. In ethnographic qualitative research, we learn how a group of people who share a common culture develop patterns of speaking and behaving and rules that govern their behavior (see Creswell, 2013). These five designs in qualitative research do not cover the full array of possible designs, but they are representative of popular approaches used in qualitative research.

- Rather than gathering numeric information, qualitative researchers gather text (e.g., audio recordings that are transcribed into words) or images (e.g., pictures taken from a camera). In fact, the hallmark of qualitative research is the extensive list of forms of data gathered, especially those becoming part of our digital age of text messages and websites. Regardless of the kinds of data collected, no scale or checklist is imposed; instead, participants are asked openly about the information they have to share, and the information is recorded.

- Analysis, then, becomes working through text passages or images one by one to form aggregated data units, first in codes, and then by collapsing the codes into themes. Sometimes the themes are interrelated to form a chronology of events, such as the process of individuals adjusting to waiting for a liver transplant (see Brown, Sorrell, McClaren, & Creswell, 2006). Qualitative software programs such as

MAXQDA (Verbi GmbH, 2013) are often used to help researchers organize, sort, and capture useful quotes.

- Because there are so many designs for qualitative research, the report format differs considerably from one qualitative study to another. The final report may range from telling a story, as in narrative designs, to a more scientific approach, as in grounded theory.
- The qualitative researcher produces a high-quality report by incorporating the views of participants, presenting a complex analysis of all of the factors involved in studying a topic or central phenomenon, ensuring that the final report is an accurate reflection of participant views (validity), and incorporating ample evidence for the codes or themes presented as results in the study. Beyond these elements would be specific criteria expected in using a particular design, such as an ethnography or a phenomenology.

Qualitative researchers in general are reluctant to set forth standards or a checklist of features that should belong in a good qualitative methods section of a study, because that would constrain emerging and creative studies. However, I think that all researchers recognize that qualitative inquirers do have certain procedures in mind when they engage in research. I have assembled a checklist of features that I feel would make a methods qualitative section complete. My qualitative checklist, like my quantitative checklist, includes elements of design and the methods of data collection and analysis (see Table 3.3).

Table 3.3 Checklist for a Complete Qualitative Methods Discussion

---

General

___ Provide a rationale for why qualitative research is well suited for studying the research problem (e.g., participant views, context, complex understanding, lack of known variables, capturing voices).

___ Describe the type of qualitative research design (e.g., narrative research, phenomenology, grounded theory, ethnography, case study) that will be used.

___ Explain why the design is well suited to address the problem.

(Conitnued)

Table 3.3 (Continued)

Qualitative data collection

___ Discuss the site(s) that will be studied.

___ Identify permissions that have been granted (include institutional review board permissions).

___ Indicate how participants will be recruited to the study.

___ Indicate the number of participants.

___ Discuss the type of purposeful sampling to be used (inclusion criteria).

___ Indicate the demographics of participants.

___ Indicate how the participants will benefit from the study (reciprocity).

___ Indicate the types of data to be collected (perhaps a table of data collection?).

___ Indicate the extent of data collection.

___ Mention the protocols (interview, observations, records) used to record the data.

___ State the research questions that will be asked (if interviews occur).

Data analysis

___ Discuss preparing the data (transcriptions).

___ Indicate the general procedure of data analysis (reading through the data and writing memos, coding the data, description, developing themes, interrelating the themes).

___ Indicate any specific procedures included in the chosen approach to the research (e.g., in grounded theory, use open coding, axial coding, and selective coding).

___ Discuss the use of qualitative data analysis software to help analyze the data (e.g., MAXQDA).

___ Discuss the use of multiple coders (i.e., intercoder agreement), if they are used in the study, and how this process was accomplished with the percentage of agreement indicated.

___ Discuss validity strategies (e.g., member checking, triangulation, negative case analysis, peer audit, external audit, immersion in the field).

___ Discuss reflexivity (how the researchers' experiences and role will influence the interpretation of findings).

Beyond these rather specific suggestions for writing a qualitative methods section, it should be mentioned that qualitative research has become accepted in the social and behavioral sciences, and it is becoming more widely used in the health sciences. In the health sciences we are seeing more and more emphasis on provider–patient interactions and learning about the choices made by patients in regard to their procedures. We are also seeing increased interest in personalized medicine, incorporating more of the human element into biological perspectives as we assess needed medical services, reaching out to diverse patient populations, and studying hospitals and clinics as organizational settings.

RECOMMENDATIONS FROM THIS CHAPTER ❖

The position I have taken is to urge mixed methods researchers to become skilled in quantitative, qualitative, and mixed methods research. Having these skills represented on mixed methods teams facilitates the development of a good mixed methods project. Collaboration on teams represents good team interactions, and it requires individuals to openly share their different methodological orientations under the guidance of a leader with diverse research skills. Individuals working independently on a mixed methods project or on a team need to know the fundamentals of the process of research. The key components of both qualitative and quantitative research need to be mastered, as do the details of writing methods sections for data collection and data analysis for each form of research. In this way, a rigorous mixed methods section can be composed that reflects solid quantitative and qualitative methods.

ADDITIONAL READINGS ❖

Brown, J., Sorrell, J. H., McClaren, J., & Creswell, J. W. (2006). Waiting for a liver transplant. *Qualitative Health Research, 16,* 119–136. doi: 10.1177/1049732305284011

Creswell, J. W. (2013). *Qualitative inquiry and research design: Choosing among five approaches* (3rd ed.). Thousand Oaks, CA: SAGE.

O'Cathain, A., Murphy, E., & Nicholl, J. (2008a). Multidisciplinary, interdisciplinary, or dysfunctional? Team working in mixed-methods research. *Qualitative Health Research, 18,* 1574–1585.

Shadish, W. R., Cook, T. D., & Campbell, D. T. (2002). *Experimental and quasi-experimental designs for generalized causal inference.* Boston, MA: Houghton Mifflin.

VERBI GmbH. (2013). MAXQDA [Computer software]. Retrieved from www.maxqda.com/

4

BASIC AND ADVANCED MIXED METHODS DESIGNS

❖ TOPICS IN THE CHAPTER

- Three basic designs and three advanced designs
- For each of these six designs, the intent of the design, the procedures of the design, a diagram of the design, and the advantages and challenges in using the design
- Criteria useful in choosing a design for your study

❖ PRELIMINARY CONSIDERATIONS

Before you identify your design, it is helpful to review the general state of research designs in the mixed methods field. There are many designs to choose from, and the names and types have multiplied over the years. Generally, I feel that mixed methods researchers develop designs that are too complicated in name and procedures. It is always helpful to start with a simple design and understand what you will accomplish by using it. Another consideration is to recognize that the designs may change after their initial conceptualization. Funding agencies may require a modified design, or the demands of resources or staff or the shifting priorities of participants in a study may require changing the design. It is best to view designs as emerging in a study and not solidly fixed in place. Finally, it is important to start with a basic design, to clearly identify the reasons for using it, and to draw a picture (or diagram) of the design. There are two general categories of designs that I will discuss: the basic designs and the advanced designs.

BASIC DESIGNS

The **basic designs** are the core designs underlying all mixed methods studies. They fall into three types: a convergent design, an explanatory sequential design, and an exploratory sequential design. In Chapters 1 and 2, I introduced these three designs. Many of the published mixed methods studies utilize one of these three designs. I always say that when looking at a published mixed methods study, you should first look for the underlying basic design being used by the author. The author may not convey this design in simple, straightforward ways, but it nonetheless does exist and is at the heart of the mixed methods study. In fact, whatever design is being used, it becomes a framework for the entire mixed methods study. Knowing your design, then, enables you to draft a title for your project, advance a mixed methods question, organize your data collection and analysis, and facilitate both the interpretation and the writing of your mixed methods study.

Basic Mixed Methods Designs

- Convergent design
- Explanatory sequential design
- Exploratory sequential design

The Convergent Design

The intent of a convergent design is to merge the results of the quantitative and qualitative data analyses. This merging then provides both a quantitative and a qualitative picture of the problem, and because both forms of data provide different insight, their combination contributes to seeing the problem from multiple angles and multiple perspectives. In short, quantitative results yield general trends and relationships, which are often needed, while qualitative results provide in-depth personal perspectives of individuals. Both are useful results, and their combination adds up to not only more data, but also a more complete understanding than what would have been provided by each database alone. This is the logic behind a convergent design. Thus, as a result of using this design, the mixed methods researcher can advance multiple perspectives or even validate one database with the other.

The **convergent design** involves the separate collection and analysis of quantitative and qualitative data. The intent is to merge the results of the quantitative and qualitative data analyses.

The procedures for using this design are straightforward:

1. Begin by collecting and analyzing the quantitative data and the qualitative data separately.

2. Merge or bring together the two databases. This can be done in several ways. After the results have been compiled, the interpretation or inferences drawn from the two databases can be brought together in a *discussion* where they are arrayed side by side. For example, the quantitative results may be reported first, followed by the qualitative results. A follow-up discussion then occurs, *comparing* the results from the two databases by displaying them one after the other (called side-by-side comparison). Another approach is **data transformation**—to transform one of the databases into the other form so that they can easily be compared. For example, counts could be made of the number of times the various themes appear in the data derived from the qualitative analysis, and these numeric values could present new variables that are entered into the quantitative database. A third way is to develop *joint displays* that array the quantitative results against the qualitative results in a table or a graph. Chapter 7 goes into more depth about creating and using these displays.

3. After the results have been merged, examine to what extent the quantitative results are confirmed by the qualitative results (or vice

versa). If they differ, then explain why these differences occurred (e.g., lack of valid quantitative measures, lack of parallel questions to facilitate data comparisons).

The convergent design is useful for researchers who need to gather both forms of data while they are in the field; it intuitively makes sense because both forms are brought together; and it enables one to gain multiple pictures of a problem from several angles. However, it is challenging to conduct. One challenge is that researchers need to start with the same measures or assessments on both the quantitative and qualitative sides if they are to merge the data. Although this parallel construction is essential, it is often overlooked. Another challenge is that researchers need to know *how* to merge the two databases. They need to be familiar with the procedures of creating joint displays or making side-by-side comparisons. How to merge the two databases—one numeric and one text based—is not intuitively clear to many researchers.

Figure 4.1 shows a simple diagram for a convergent design. This rendering is where researchers should begin when they start drawing a diagram of the procedures for their design. I call this design a single-phase design because both forms of data are collected at the same time.

The Explanatory Sequential Design

The intent of the explanatory sequential design is to study a problem by beginning with a quantitative **strand** (a *strand* refers to either the

Figure 4.1   Convergent Design

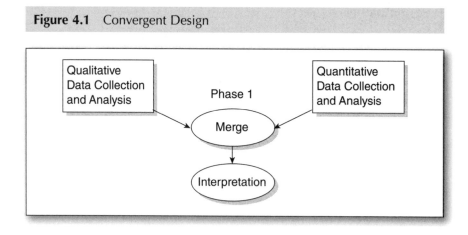

quantitative or qualitative component of a study) to both collect and analyze data, and then to conduct qualitative research to explain the quantitative results. Quantitative results yield statistical significance, confidence intervals, and effect sizes and provide the general outcomes of a study. However, when we obtain such results, we often do not know how the findings occurred. Therefore, we engage in a qualitative phase to help explain the quantitative research results. Hence, this design is called an explanatory sequential design.

> The intent of the **explanatory sequential design** is to begin with a quantitative strand and then conduct a second qualitative strand to explain the quantitative results.

Conduct this design by following these procedures:

1. Collect and analyze quantitative data in the first phase.

2. Examine the results of the quantitative analysis to determine (a) what results will need further exploration in the second, qualitative phase and (b) what questions to ask participants in this qualitative phase.

3. Conduct qualitative data collection and analysis in a second phase to help explain the quantitative results.

4. Draw inferences about how the qualitative results help to explain the quantitative results.

The strength of this design lies in the fact that the two phases build upon each other so that there are distinct, easily recognized stages of conducting the design. Because of this, the design is popular among beginning mixed methods researchers and graduate students. It is also popular among researchers who have a quantitative background, because the study begins with a quantitative phase. It is challenging to conduct, however, because it takes time to implement two distinct phases in sequence. Another challenge is determining which quantitative results need further explanation. Choices for the researcher include following up on participants with certain demographics, expanding the investigation to explain important variables (or variables that surprisingly turned out to be nonsignificant), and looking closely at outlier cases from the quantitative results.

Figure 4.2 provides a simple diagram of the procedures in the two-phase explanatory sequential design.

Figure 4.2 Explanatory Sequential Design

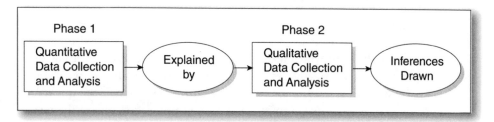

The Exploratory Sequential Design

The intent of the exploratory sequential design is to study a problem by first exploring it through qualitative data collection and analysis. After this first phase, a second phase involves taking the qualitative results and developing them into measures or a new instrument or new interventions for an experiment. This second, quantitative phase is then followed by a third, quantitative phase of applying the measures, testing the new instrument, or using the new intervention and its activities in an experiment. As you can see, there are several possibilities for the third quantitative phase.

> The intent of the **exploratory sequential design** is to first explore a problem through qualitative data collection and analysis, develop an instrument or intervention, and follow with a third quantitative phase.

To conduct this design, follow these procedures:

1. Collect and analyze the qualitative data.

2. Examine the results from the qualitative analysis (e.g., the themes) and use the information to design a quantitative component, such as new measures, new instruments, or new intervention activities. The idea is that the new quantitative component improves on what is already available (e.g., an existing instrument) because it is grounded in the actual experiences of participants.

3. Use the new quantitative component and test it out. This means that the new measures will be put into an existing quantitative database. It may mean that the new instrument is tested for the validity and reliability of its scores. It may also mean that a new element is placed into an experimental trial and used as part of the intervention (or as new pre- and post-test measures).

4. The final step, then, is to report how the new component (e.g., measures, instruments, or activities) improves upon the existing set of variables, provides a new and better contextualized instrument, or adds helpful activities into the intervention so that it enhances the workability of the intervention. In addition, because the qualitative data are drawn from a small sample in the first phase, the test of the new quantitative component can provide insight into whether the initial qualitative results can be generalized to a large sample in the third quantitative phase.

As you can see, there are three major steps in this design: initial qualitative phase, second quantitative phase, and third quantitative phase. I call it a three-phase design. With three phases, it also becomes the most difficult of the three basic designs. Like the explanatory sequential design, this design takes time, but these phases are extended out in time much more than the other basic designs. This design is also challenging to conduct because of the difficulty in taking qualitative results and turning them into a new variable, a new instrument, or a new set of intervention activities.

What can be taken from the qualitative results to facilitate these processes? Qualitative results yield specific quotes from individuals, codes as aggregations of quotes, and themes as the collection of codes. When new measures are developed in this design, themes could be transitioned into measures or variables. When a new instrument is needed, the quotes could become items; the codes, variables; and the themes, scales. When new intervention activities become the outcome of the qualitative phase, these activities could be directed by both codes and themes. A further challenge of this design—when developing a new instrument or modifying an existing one based on the qualitative results—is the development of a good instrument with strong psychometric properties. There are many sources for good scale development and instrument construction (e.g., DeVellis, 2012). I have also developed my own list of steps:

1. Review the literature / obtain expert panel advice.

2. Identify possible items.

3. Pretest the items with a small sample using exploratory factor analysis.

4. Conduct reliability analysis of the scales.

5. Administer the survey to a large sample.

6. Conduct confirmatory factor analysis of the results.

7. Use structural equation modeling to identify latent variables.

8. Look for evidence of construct validity.

On the positive side, this design's rigor makes it a sophisticated mixed methods design. Further, because the first phase is exploratory, this design is useful in mixed methods studies in underdeveloped countries (and studies of global health), where the measures drawn from the world of Western research may have little applicability and researchers need to first explore what measures will work in the setting. Also, researchers comfortable and familiar with qualitative research like this design because it begins with a qualitative phase.

A diagram for an exploratory sequential design is shown in Figure 4.3. As you can see, this design has three connected phases:

Figure 4.3   Exploratory Sequential Design

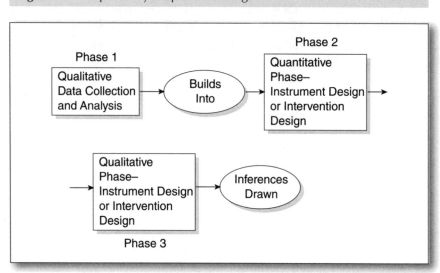

ADVANCED DESIGNS   ❖

As I have said, the place to begin to think about mixed methods designs is to identify the basic design in your project. From this basic design, you then build out into other designs—or **advanced designs**, as I call them. In an advanced design, something is added to the basic design. I will illustrate in this chapter three additions that are popular in the mixed methods literature: the intervention design, the social justice design, and the multistage evaluation design. Within each of these advanced designs, we can find a basic design.

Advanced Mixed Methods Designs

- Intervention design
- Social justice design
- Multistage evaluation design

The Intervention Design

The intent of the intervention design is to study a problem by conducting an experiment or an intervention trial and adding qualitative data into it.

An experiment or intervention consists of identifying multiple groups (e.g., control and experimental groups), testing a treatment with the experimental group, and determining if the treatment has an effect on the outcomes. The control group, not receiving the treatment, should not change in terms of the outcome. Within this pre- and post-test model with an experimental intervention, we can place qualitative data. This qualitative data can serve a number of purposes, and mixed methods researchers think about adding the data into the experiment before the experiment begins, during the experiment, or after the experiment. (Of course, it can be added into the experiment at all three times, depending on resources and the objectives of the trial.) It can be added into the experiment *before* the experiment begins for the purpose of, for example, recruiting individuals to the trial by conducting interviews, or to help design the intervention procedures that may likely impact participants in the experiment. In this case, the researcher is using an exploratory sequential basic design within an intervention trial because the qualitative exploration precedes the trial. Qualitative data can be added in *during* the experiment to study how participants are experiencing the intervention activities and whether these activities might have negative or positive implications for the trial. In this case, the researcher is using a convergent design because the qualitative data flows into the trial at the same time the quantitative trial is under way. Or the qualitative data can be added into the trial *after* the experiment is over in order to follow up on the outcomes and help explain them in more detail than the statistical results alone yield. This would constitute using an explanatory sequential basic design within the intervention design.

> The **intervention design** adds to one of the basic designs. The intent is to study a problem by conducting an experiment or an intervention trial and adding qualitative data into it.

To conduct this design, follow these procedures:

1. Determine how qualitative data will be used in the experiment or intervention trial according to the basic design: before (exploratory sequential), during (convergent), or after (explanatory).

2. Conduct the experiment: Assign groups to control and treatment; determine pre- and post-test measures; gather the data; and assess whether the treatment had an effect.

3. Analyze the qualitative results to determine their impact.

4. Interpret how the qualitative results enhanced the experimental results.

This design is challenging because the researcher needs to know how to run a rigorous experiment that employs standards such as random assignment, a high quality of "dosage" of the treatment, controls for threats to validity, and so forth (see Creswell, 2012). It is also challenging because the researcher needs to determine where to collect qualitative data in the process of research, and whether to gather qualitative data at multiple points in the design. When investigators gather qualitative data during the experiment, researcher bias needs to be closely monitored so that the intrusion of qualitative data collection does not unduly influence the outcomes in the trial. In some cases the investigators gather what is called unobtrusive data (e.g., journals kept by participants *during* the trial) after the trial concludes. On the positive side, this design is a rigorous one and popular in the health sciences, where the randomized controlled trial is the gold standard for research. In many articles, authors are critical of experimental trials, and this design adds elements into the trial that make the results more believable and factor the human element into laboratory-contrived research studies.

There are many ways to draw a diagram of the procedures for an intervention mixed methods design. One simple illustration would be to position the additional data before, during, or after the experiment, as shown in Figure 4.4.

Figure 4.4   Intervention Design

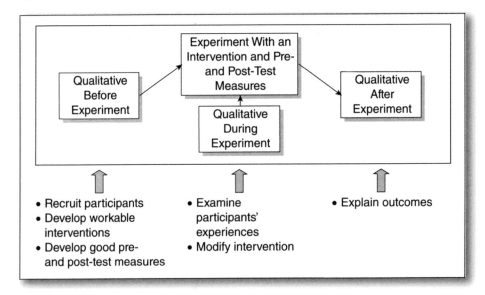

The Social Justice Design

The intent of a social justice design is to study a problem within an overall social justice framework that threads throughout the mixed methods study. Several possible frameworks can be found in mixed methods projects: a gender lens (feminist or masculine), a racial or ethnic lens, a social class lens, a disability lens, a lifestyle orientation lens, or any combination of lenses. At the center of these mixed methods studies would be a basic design (convergent, explanatory sequential, or exploratory sequential), but the investigator would include the social justice lens throughout the study.

How would the lens be threaded through the study? For example, as shown in Figure 4.5, we see a mixed methods study with an explanatory sequential basic design. But inserted in at many points in the design are aspects of feminist theory. The theory is established at the beginning of the study, informs the type of research questions asked, shapes the types of participants (women), finds a presence in both data collection and the reporting of themes, and prompts a call to action—a change—at the end of the study.

Figure 4.5 Social Justice Design

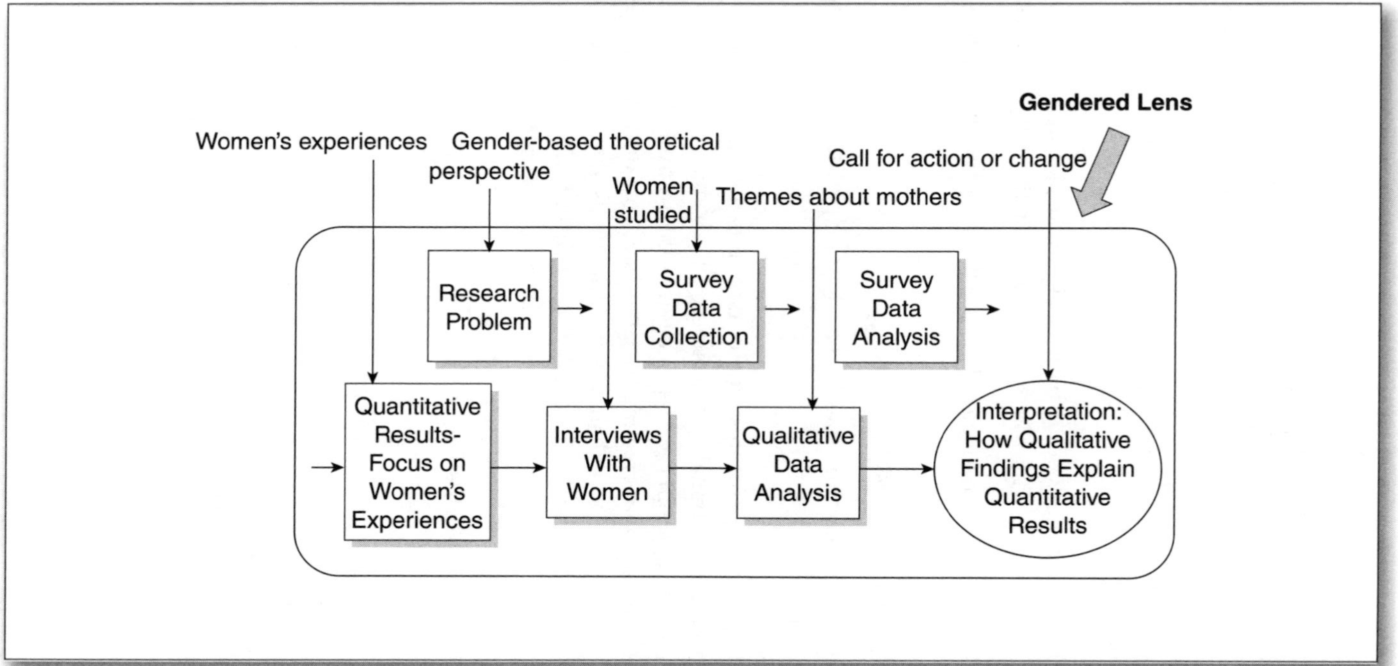

> The intent of the **social justice design** is to study a problem within an overall social justice framework. The researcher adds to the basic design by threading this framework throughout the mixed methods study.

The procedures involved in this type of mixed methods design are as follows:

1. Identify the type of basic design you plan on using, and consider where and why you are adding qualitative data to the study.

2. Include the theoretical lens to inform many (if not all) of the phases in the design.

3. Conduct the study.

4. Discuss how the social justice lens helped address the situation being studied.

The advantage of this type of design is that the outcomes are intended to help a marginalized group or disadvantaged individuals. The call for change comes in the final section of the study, in which the researcher takes a stand about creating social justice. This design is popular in countries around the world in which individuals live in a state of injustice and marginalization. The challenges in using this design lie in deciding what social justice lens to use, how to incorporate it in many phases of the study, and how to include it in such a way that it does not further marginalize participants.

The Multistage Evaluation Design

The intent of the multistage evaluation design is to conduct a study over time that evaluates the success of a program or activities implemented into a setting. It is called "multistage" because each one of its components can represent a single study itself. It becomes evaluative when the overall intent is to assess the merit, value, or worth of a program or set of activities. The separate projects that constitute the overall evaluation design can be quantitative, qualitative, or mixed methods. As with other advanced designs, within these studies would be parts that reflect a convergent, explanatory sequential, or exploratory sequential design.

The intent of the **multistage evaluation design** is to conduct a study over time that evaluates the success of a program or activities implemented into a setting.

Figure 4.6 illustrates the many phases, both quantitative and qualitative, that go into developing and testing measures, implementing the program, and conducting follow-up.

To conduct this design, follow these procedures:

1. Identify what program needs to be evaluated and the team members who will conduct it.

2. Consider which basic design is needed for the evaluation. Typically, evaluations begin with a needs assessment and an exploratory sequential design.

3. Identify the stages in the evaluation. These might include a needs assessment, theory conceptualization, specification of measures and instruments, testing out the program using the measures and instruments, and follow-up to help explain the program implementation test.

Figure 4.6 Multistage Evaluation Design

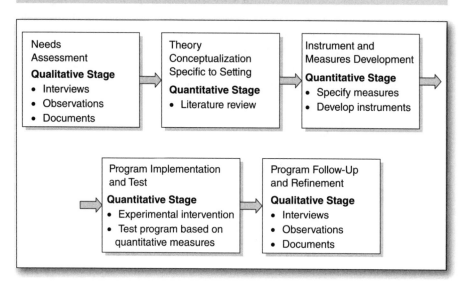

4. Determine at each phase whether quantitative or qualitative data or both will be collected and analyzed.

5. Conduct the evaluation, and revise the program and instruments if needed.

The strength of the multiphase evaluation design lies in its systematic procedures for documenting the success of a program. It can involve team members who have both quantitative and qualitative (or mixed methods) skills. It is also a complex type of design, conducted over time, that would be seen by funding agencies as a rigorous, multifaceted project.

One challenge for using this design is that it is not suitable for the "single" researcher but requires a team to conduct the study (often with the support of stakeholders). Finding funding and time for researchers to engage in this type of project may be difficult. Also, team members need to be coordinated to facilitate their working together and to ensure clarity about the overall evaluation goal of the project. Finally, one stage leads to another, so the team needs to consider how one stage contributes to the next stage. This flow of activities requires strong team leadership (see Chapter 3).

❖ HOW TO CHOOSE A DESIGN

I would recommend that you begin by identifying your basic design. To select a basic design, I would consider whether you plan to merge the two databases or connect them. This will lead down the path to either a *convergent* design (merging the data) or a *sequential* design (connecting the data). Then I would discuss whether something will be added to the design, such as an experiment, a social justice lens, or a long-term evaluation element. These factors will push the basic design into an advanced design.

Other factors play into your selection of a design. I would consider the skills and orientation that you bring to mixed methods research. If your background resides in a stronger quantitative orientation (either through personal interest or the discipline of your field), then I would urge you toward a design that starts with quantitative research (i.e., an explanatory sequential design). If you have an orientation toward qualitative research, I would suggest that you consider more of an exploratory sequential design that begins with qualitative research. I would also assess whether your skills are stronger in quantitative research than in qualitative, or vice versa.

Finally, I would recommend that you look into the literature in your field to see what types of mixed methods designs are being used. When my colleague and I reviewed mixed methods empirical investigations in the trauma research field, we found mostly explanatory sequential designs (Creswell & Zhang, 2009). When I have participated in discussions about mixed methods projects in the health sciences, I have found intervention designs with qualitative data added before, during, or after the experiment (Creswell, Fetters, Plano Clark, & Morales, 2009).

RECOMMENDATIONS FROM THIS CHAPTER ❖

The following are specific recommendations that flow from ideas in this chapter:

- In your initial thinking about a design for your mixed methods study, consider one of the three basic designs. Probably the easiest to execute would be the explanatory sequential design, followed by the convergent design, and then the exploratory sequential design. This last design is more complicated because it requires more phases in the study, and it requires a wide array of skills.
- Start thinking about your design not from the standpoint of timing (what comes first, what comes second) or emphasis (whether qualitative or quantitative has greater emphasis in your project), but rather based on *intent*, what you hope to accomplish with the design and your questions. Do you intend to compare the two databases (convergent design)? To explain quantitative results with qualitative data (explanatory sequential design)? To explore first and then build in a quantitative component to your study (exploratory sequential design)?
- After deciding on your basic design, consider whether you will add features that extend your basic design into an advanced design. Will you add an experiment (or intervention trial)? A social justice framework? A program evaluation?
- Choose your design based on these factors: the intent (what you hope to accomplish), your background and skill level, and the orientation toward design found in your field or discipline.

❖ ADDITIONAL READINGS

Regarding the mixed methods designs, see:

Creswell, J. W., & Plano Clark, V. L. (2011). *Designing and conducting mixed methods research* (2nd ed.). Thousand Oaks, CA: SAGE.

Regarding experimental designs, see:

Creswell, J. W. (2012). *Educational research: Planning, conducting, and evaluating quantitative and qualitative research*. Boston, MA: Pearson.

Shadish, W. R., Cook, T. D., & Campbell, D. T. (2002). *Experimental and quasi-experimental designs for generalized causal inference*. Boston, MA: Houghton Mifflin.

Regarding general evaluation designs, see:

Rossi, P. H., Lipsey, M. W., & Freeman, H. E. (2004). *Evaluation: A systematic approach*. Thousand Oaks, CA: SAGE.

Regarding instrument or scale design, see:

DeVellis, R. F. (2012). *Scale development: Theory and applications* (3rd ed.). Thousand Oaks, CA: SAGE.

For good examples of the types of designs that I would recommend, see:

(Convergent design)
Wittink, M. N., Barg, F. K., & Gallo, J. J. (2006). Unwritten rules of talking to doctors about depression: Integrating qualitative and quantitative methods. *Annals of Family Medicine, 4,* 302–309. doi: 10.1370/afm.558.

(Explanatory sequential design)
Ivankova, N. V., & Stick, S. L. (2007). Students' persistence in a distributed doctoral program in educational leadership in higher education: A mixed methods study. *Research in Higher Education, 48,* 93–135. doi: 10.1007/s11162-006-9025-4.

(Exploratory sequential design)
Betancourt, T. S., Meyers-Ohki, S. E., Stevenson, A., Ingabire, C., Kanyanganzi, F., Munyana, M., . . . Beardslee, W. R. (2011). Using mixed-methods research to adapt and evaluate a family strengthening intervention in Rwanda. *African Journal of Traumatic Stress, 2*(1), 32–45.

(Intervention design)
Rogers, A., Day, J., Randall, F., & Bentall, R. P. (2003). Patients' understanding and participation in a trial designed to improve the management of anti-psychotic medication: A qualitative study. *Social Psychiatry and Psychiatric Epidemiology, 38*(12), 720–727. doi: 10.1007/s00127-003-0693-5.

(Social justice design)
Hodgkin, S. (2008). Telling it all: A story of women's social capital using a mixed methods approach. *Journal of Mixed Methods Research, 2*(4), 296–316. doi:10.1177/1558689808321641.

(Multistage evaluation design)
Nastasi, B. K., Hitchcock, J., Sarkar, S., Burkholder, G., Varjas, K., & Jayasena, A. (2007). Mixed methods in intervention research: Theory to adaptation. *Journal of Mixed Methods Research, 1*(2), 164–182. doi: 10.1177/1558689806298181

CHAPTER 5

HOW TO DRAW A DIAGRAM OF PROCEDURES

TOPICS IN THE CHAPTER

- Definition and use of diagrams in mixed methods research
- Tools for drawing diagrams
- Basic steps in drawing a diagram
- Sample diagrams for the basic and advanced mixed methods designs

DEFINITION OF A DIAGRAM

Within the context of mixed methods research, a **diagram of procedures** is a figure that is used to convey the procedures used in a mixed methods design. It includes information about the data collection, the data analysis, and the interpretation of a study. It may be unusual to think about having a procedural diagram in a study, but we do have diagrams for the theories that we use in studies. When our procedures are complex—such as in mixed methods, where there are multiple quantitative and qualitative data collection and analysis steps—it is helpful to have a visual diagram to pull together all of the components of the study. Added to this is that mixed methods might be hard to understand because it is new, and an overview of the procedures can be useful to listeners and readers.

❖ THE USE OF DIAGRAMS

Around 2003, a visit with a federal funding program officer led to the development of diagrams for mixed methods procedures. This officer liked mixed methods studies, but said that they were difficult to understand because of the multiple components of data collection and analysis. After that conversation, my colleagues and I began developing diagrams of our mixed methods procedures, and we have continued to elaborate and develop them ever since. They have multiple uses. Graduate students can begin with their diagram as they launch into a discussion about their proposed mixed methods study. These diagrams are beginning to appear in mixed methods journals, such as the *Journal of Mixed Methods Research*. They are also being included in applications or proposals for funding, and they become helpful visuals during presentations of mixed methods studies at conferences.

In short, diagrams summarize much information in a short space, and have multiple possibilities for application.

❖ TOOLS FOR DRAWING DIAGRAMS

To draw a figure, you need a computer program—if the figure is to be published or presented to an audience. Many mixed methods researchers use PowerPoint to draw a figure because of the ease of placing material on a page. Others might use a word processing program, or even compose a figure using a spreadsheet program. Of course, there are also specific computer drawing programs that might be used.

Before drawing your diagram, it is necessary to know the type of design that you will include in your study and whether it is a basic or advanced design. Further, using a notation system that is familiar to mixed methods researchers will enhance your diagram.

❖ NOTATIONS FOR DIAGRAMS

In 1991, Morse was the first author to begin to specify the notation system that has become popular in mixed methods research. In Table 5.1, you can see the basic notation that has developed. It is certainly employed unevenly in mixed methods studies, but the plus sign (+) and the right arrow (→) have become standard features to signify that the quantitative and qualitative

Table 5.1   Notation for Mixed Methods Diagrams

Notation	What It Indicates	Example	Key Citations
Uppercase letters	Prioritized methods	QUAN, QUAL	Morse (1991, 2003)
Lowercase letters	Lesser priority	quan, qual	Morse (1991, 2003)
+	Convergent methods	QUAN + QUAL	Morse (1991, 2003)
→	Sequential methods	QUAN→QUAL	Morse (1991, 2003)

methods are being added together or that one follows the other. Thus, these are two symbols that you are likely to encounter in diagrams. Less used are some of the other symbols, such as uppercase letters to indicate priority or emphasis of the quantitative or qualitative strand of the study and lowercase letters to indicate less priority or emphasis. Other symbols include parentheses, which are used to embed information, and brackets, which indicate individual studies within a series of studies. The idea of including notation has perhaps fallen out of favor in recent years in order to simplify the diagrams and not clutter them with information.

ESSENTIAL ELEMENTS IN A DIAGRAM   ❖

Back in 2006, Ivankova, Creswell, and Stick assembled key ideas that guide what goes into a diagram. Five parts are essential:

1. Boxes that show the data collection and analysis for both quantitative and qualitative research.

2. A circle that shows the interpretation phase of a study.

3. Procedures that attach to both the data collection and analysis phases of both quantitative and qualitative research. These are shown as bulleted points positioned alongside the boxes.

4. Products that will result from each phase of data collection and analysis (represented by bullets positioned alongside the boxes).

5. Arrows that show the sequence of procedures.

Other features are important as well.

Essential Elements in a Procedural Diagram

- Boxes indicate data collection and analysis.
- Circles indicate integration and interpretation.
- Procedures are briefly described with text.
- Products are briefly described with text.
- Arrows indicate the sequence of procedures

Title

The diagram or figure needs to have a title that conveys the type of design being used. For example, you might frame the title this way:

Figure 1. A Convergent Design of the Mixed Methods Study of Adolescent Smoking Behavior.

This title mentions the type of design as well as the key intent or focus of the study.

Vertical or Horizontal Orientation

The diagram can be drawn either vertically or horizontally on the page. Typically, the convergent design is drawn vertically and sequential designs are drawn horizontally. Writers need to consider their audience for these diagrams to determine what would be most appropriate. For example, most diagrams drawn for studies in the military or in the health sciences are drawn vertically to match the top-down structure found in these organizations.

Simplicity

Another consideration is whether to label the information in the boxes as "Data collection" or "Data analysis," or to include a more complete description, such as "Interview data collection" or "Interview data collection with 20 adolescents." Individuals new to mixed methods often include more complete information and detail in the boxes in a diagram. These individuals may have more of a "content" orientation to the drawing than a "methods" orientation, and develop the diagram to tell as much about the content of the study as the specific methods procedures.

A key idea in drawing a diagram is not to overdraw it, but to keep it simple and straightforward. Thus, many different arrows going many directions would not be recommended, and the simple configuration of data collection, data analysis, and interpretation for both the quantitative and qualitative strand would be advised.

Single Page

The diagram needs to fit on a single page. This approach conserves space as well as facilitates reading the diagram. Having to follow arrows or boxes from one page to another is often confusing.

Timeline

It is often helpful to assign times to different phases of the research. When will data collection occur? Data analysis? Interpretation? The timeline in months or days can be placed on a line that runs alongside the boxes in the diagram. It helps readers as well as the researcher understand when the phases of the project will occur.

BASIC STEPS IN DRAWING A DIAGRAM   ❖

1. Select a drawing program to use.

2. Draw the basic design that you plan on using: a convergent design, an explanatory design, or an exploratory design. Use boxes to indicate data collection and data analysis, use circles to indicate interpretation, and use arrows to indicate the flow of procedures.

3. Add in features that signify an advanced design, such as by placing a framework around the basic design and labeling it for its advanced features.

4. Add additional information into the diagram: the procedures, the product, the timeline, the phases, and color coding, if you like.

VISUAL MODELS OF DIAGRAMS BY DESIGN   ❖

Look at Figure 5.1 to see diagrams of the three basic designs: a convergent parallel design, an explanatory sequential design, and an exploratory sequential design. As you can see, each diagram consists of boxes for data collection and data analysis, and circles for interpretation for both the quantitative

Figure 5.1 Procedural Diagrams for the Basic Mixed Methods Designs

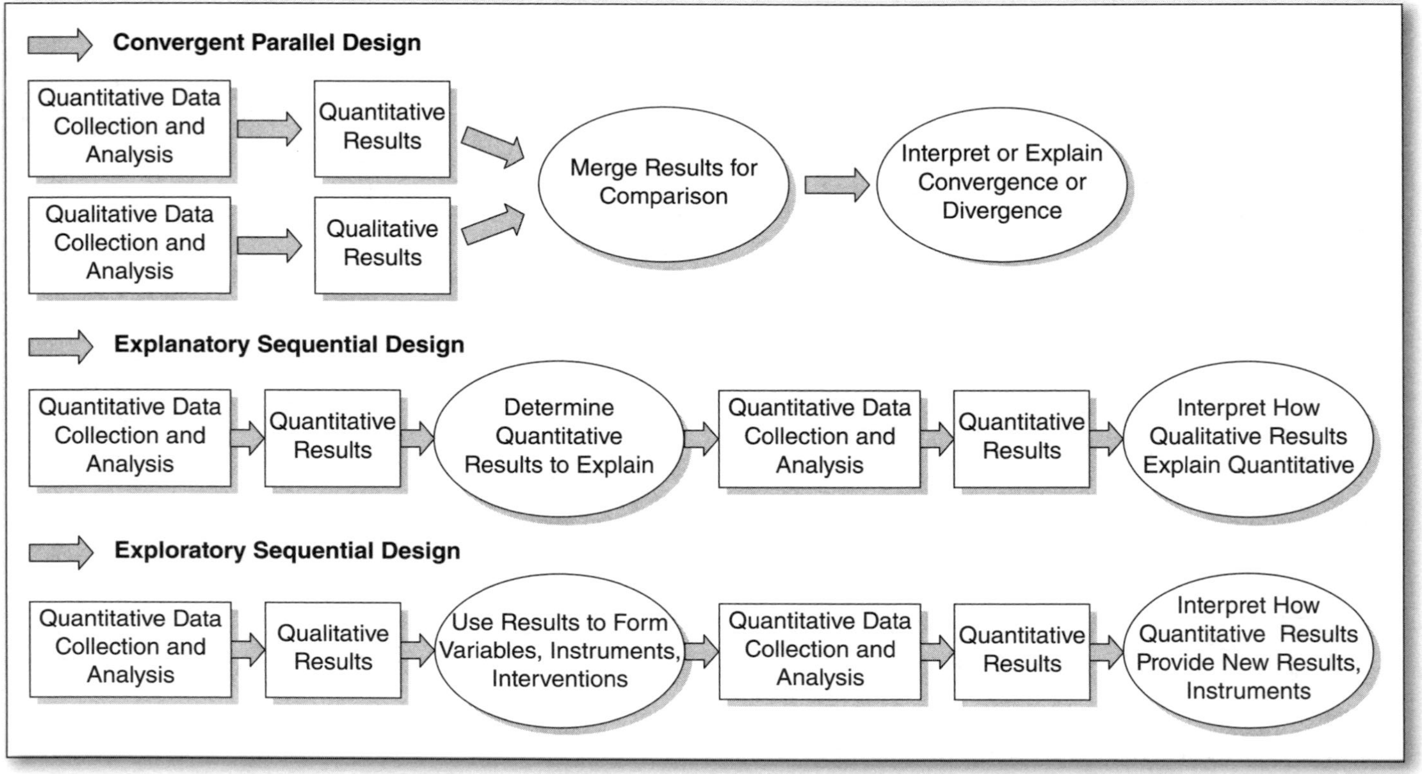

Convergent Parallel Design

Quantitative Data Collection and Analysis → Quantitative Results

Qualitative Data Collection and Analysis → Qualitative Results

→ Merge Results for Comparison → Interpret or Explain Convergence or Divergence

Explanatory Sequential Design

Quantitative Data Collection and Analysis → Quantitative Results → Determine Quantitative Results to Explain → Quantitative Data Collection and Analysis → Quantitative Results → Interpret How Qualitative Results Explain Quantitative

Exploratory Sequential Design

Quantitative Data Collection and Analysis → Qualitative Results → Use Results to Form Variables, Instruments, Interventions → Quantitative Data Collection and Analysis → Quantitative Results → Interpret How Quantitative Results Provide New Results, Instruments and qualitative research. Arrows indicate the flow of activities, and all three diagrams are drawn (for convenience) in horizontal fashion. Words are inserted into the diagrams to briefly describe the method steps in each design.

Figure 5.2, showing diagrams of the advanced designs, provides useful models for designing a mixed methods intervention study, social justice study, or multistage evaluation study.

Into the basic designs, we can add features that provide additional information. Look at Figure 5.3. This figure lists the procedures, presented as bullets alongside the major boxes. It also lists the products in the middle of the diagram, and includes a timeline along the outside of the diagram. A title indicating that this is a convergent design is displayed at the bottom of the diagram to reflect APA style format. Further, as a convergent design, this design is identified as a single-phase design.

An explanatory sequential design is shown in Figure 5.4. Here we see a horizontal design with boxes, procedures and products that relate to the boxes, a timeline, a two-phase designation, and a title.

ADDING PROCEDURES ❖
AND PRODUCTS IN DIAGRAMS

As shown in these diagrams, the procedures and products are earmarked with bullets, and the amount of information that can be inserted is quite limited. This means that the researcher needs to consider what is most important when deciding which information to supply in the bulleted points.

Table 5.2 illustrates the types of data that could be provided in the diagrams for both quantitative data collection and analysis and qualitative data collection and analysis. *Procedures* refer to the steps or methods the researcher undertakes during each phase of the study, while *products* indicate specific outcomes that results at each stage. Products are especially helpful to have in making reports to federal, state, and public agencies about the specific outcomes of a project.

DRAWING ADVANCED DESIGNS DIAGRAMS ❖

Often it is helpful to see the basic design before drawing the advanced design. For example, in an intervention advanced design, the basic design might be the experiment followed by interviews to explain the experimental

Figure 5.2 Procedural Diagrams for the Advanced Mixed Methods Designs

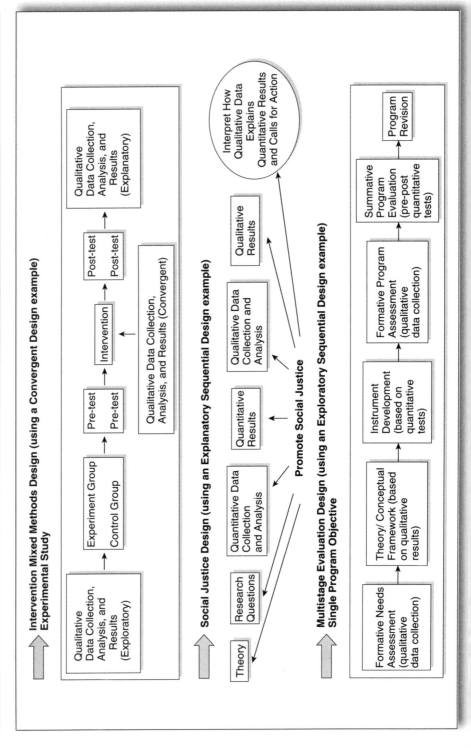

58

Figure 5.3 A Convergent Mixed Methods Design of _____

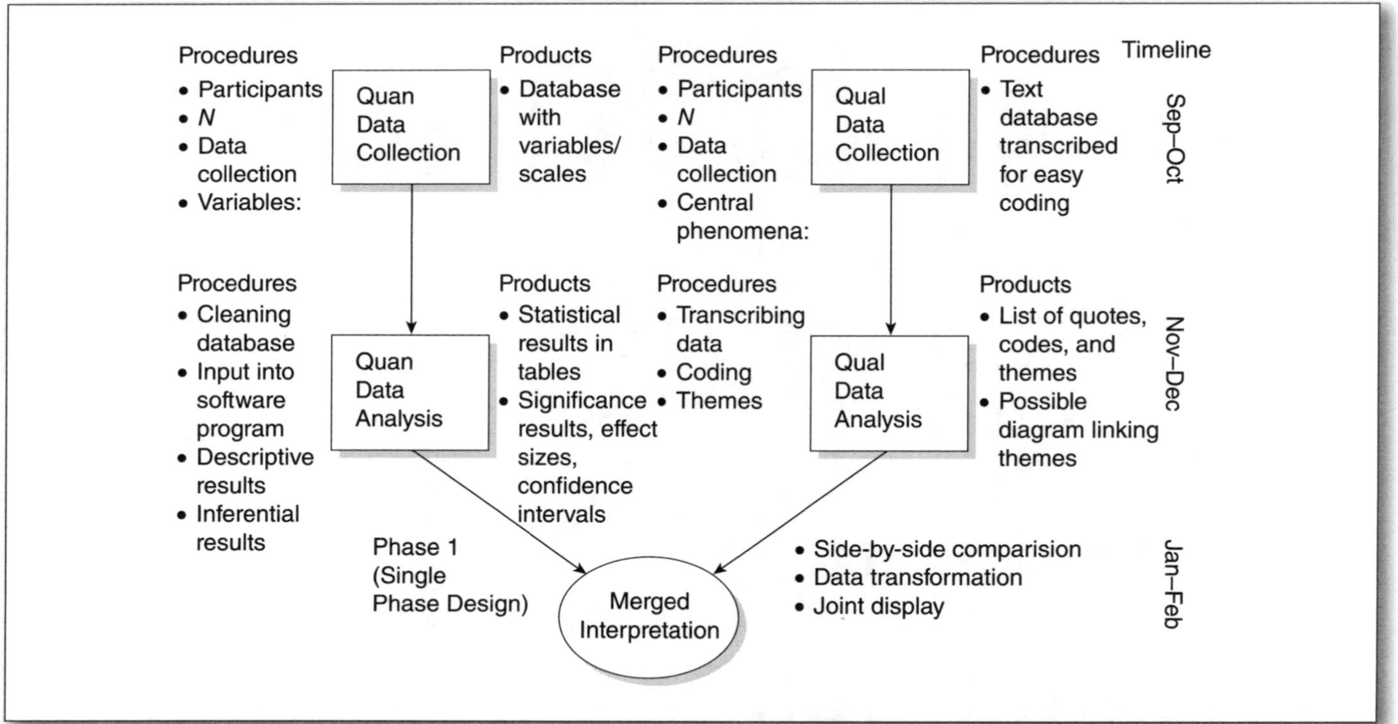

Timeline

Sep–Oct

Nov–Dec

Jan–Feb

Procedures
- Participants
- *N*
- Data collection
- Variables:

Quan Data Collection

Products
- Database with variables/ scales

Procedures
- Participants
- *N*
- Data collection
- Central phenomena:

Qual Data Collection

Products
- List of quotes, codes, and themes
- Possible diagram linking themes

Procedures
- Text database transcribed for easy coding

Procedures
- Cleaning database
- Input into software program
- Descriptive results
- Inferential results

Quan Data Analysis

Products
- Statistical results in tables
- Significance results, effect sizes, confidence intervals

Procedures
- Transcribing data
- Coding
- Themes

Qual Data Analysis

- Side-by-side comparision
- Data transformation
- Joint display

Merged Interpretation

Phase 1 (Single Phase Design)

Figure 5.4 An Explanatory Sequential Mixed Methods Design of _____

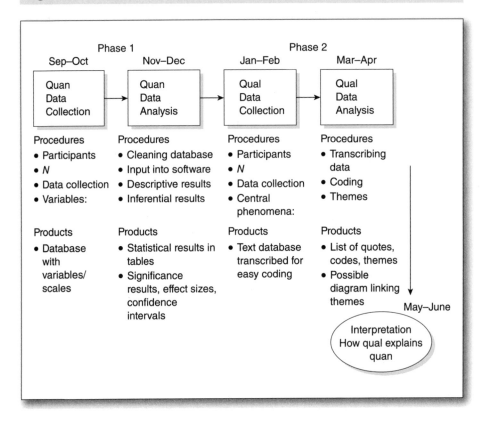

Table 5.2 Information for Procedures and Products in a Diagram

	Procedures	Products
Quantitative data collection	• Participants • N • Data collection • Variables=	• Database with variables/ scales
Quantitative data analysis	• Clean database • Input into software program • Descriptive results • Inferential results	• Statistical results in tables • Significance results, effect sizes, confidence intervals

	Procedures	Products
Qualitative data collection	• Participants • *N* • Data collection • Central phenomena	• Text database transcribed for easy coding
Qualitative data analysis	• Transcribing data • Coding • Themes	• List of quotes, codes, and theme • Possible diagram linking themes

findings. To picture an advanced design might require two figures, one of them for the basic design, as illustrated in Figure 5.5. This design would then be followed by a more complete design that indicates procedures, products, a timeline, and phases, as shown in Figure 5.6, which shows an explanatory sequential basic design encased within an experimental, intervention design. The qualitative strand of the project follows the experiment and helps to explain the experimental results.

RECOMMENDATIONS FROM THIS CHAPTER   ❖

In conclusion, I would recommend that a diagram always be included with a mixed methods study. This diagram provides a useful overview of the procedures and helps readers understand complex features of the design. Further, I have reviewed several basic features in drawing these diagrams.

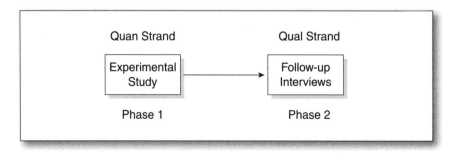

Figure 5.5   Advanced Design: Intervention Design (With Explanatory Sequential Basic Design)

Figure 5.6 An Intervention Mixed Methods Design of _____

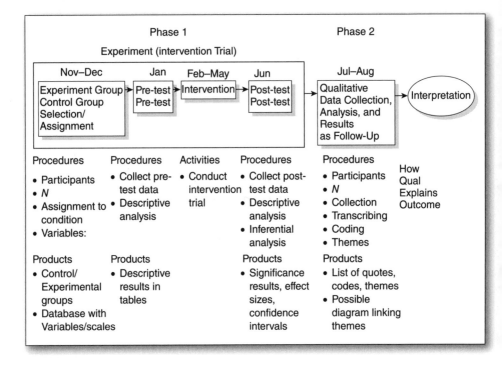

Most importantly, I recommend keeping the diagram simple, straightforward, and located on a single page. When drawing the diagram, always begin with the basic design, and then add in the advanced design features when needed. Further details can be incorporated into the design to provide more information to engage the reader.

❖ ADDITIONAL READINGS

Ivankova, N. V., Creswell, J. W., & Stick, S. (2006). Using mixed methods sequential explanatory design: From theory to practice. *Field Methods, 18,* 3–20.

Morse, J. M. (1991). Approaches to qualitative-quantitative methodological triangulation. *Nursing Research, 40,* 120–123.

CHAPTER 6

INTRODUCING A MIXED METHODS STUDY

THE IMPORTANCE OF ❖
A GOOD INTRODUCTION

One of the most important aspects of any research study is the introduction. If authors do not catch the reader in the first few paragraphs of a study, they are likely to lose their audience before the project even begins. This opening section must create a problem or issue that needs to be addressed, convince the reader of the importance of this issue, and signal how important it is to come up with potential solutions to this problem. Novelists know this approach well. They invite the reader into a dilemma at the outset and then provide enough clues as the pages proceed to give readers the feeling that they are inching ever closer to solving or at least learning about the problem. Similarly, composers create chords with dissonance and then resolve that dissonance with pleasing chords. Sitcom producers often string along two or three major dilemmas, hoping at the end of the half-hour program to bring them all to a satisfactory conclusion, either in tandem or individually. Thus, this model of research—creating a problem or issue that will subsequently be addressed—is not new and is familiar to us in many realms of our lives.

❖ A SCRIPT FOR WRITING A MIXED METHODS INTRODUCTION

For several years, the importance of following a script outlining the components of an introduction has been emphasized in research methods books (see Creswell, 2014, on "Research Design"). This script has been called a "social science deficiency" model for writing an introduction to a study, but it applies equally to the health sciences. An introduction to a study is intended to spark readers' interest in the subject, specify a problem or issue that needs to be addressed, convey the specific aim (or purpose) of the study, and, in many cases, narrow the specific aim (or purpose) down to specific research questions. The template for an introduction that I often see in rigorous studies in the social, behavioral, and health sciences has five sections.

Writing an Introduction

1. The topic

2. The problem

3. The existing literature

4. Deficiencies in the literature

5. Audiences that will profit

Following these five sections are the purpose statement (or study aim) and the research questions. The five sections are described below.

The Topic

The first couple of sentences set the general topic for the study, such as depression screening or adolescent behavior in middle schools. Give references, cite statistics, and let the reader know that this is an important topic for consideration. Also give some attention to the first sentence, which colleagues in literature call a "narrative hook." In the first one or two sentences, it is important to grab your readers and compel them to read on. Finally, give readers a topic that they can relate to, not something esoteric that will cause them to ponder and linger over the opening sentences. This might be referred to as "lowering the reader down into the well slowly."

The Problem

After introducing the topic, it is important to create a clear picture of the problem or issue that needs to be addressed by the research. This is a difficult passage to write, and many researchers refer to "what is being done" rather than creating an issue or concern. What problem needs to be solved or addressed? You might also think about this issue as one arising out of practice: In the health clinic, what is the issue in scheduling? In the community, what is the issue in getting people involved? Often researchers cite only the literature issue—"the lack of research"—and leave it at that. Certainly, not having studies on the problem is important, but what are the consequences of (if you will, what is the matter with) not having studies? Further, there may be multiple problems leading to a need for a study. Mention all of them. Also, provide citations to support your claims about the problem. This becomes good scholarly research.

The Existing Literature

Next, convey the existing literature that has attempted to address the problem. This section is not a literature review, but a general survey of the groups of studies that have addressed the problem. For some problems, literature may be nonexistent. For other problems, many studies may exist, but they may not speak squarely to the direction being taken in your study. Be sure to give citations in this section. Reference enough of the literature so that the reader can conclude that you have thoroughly looked over the literature and cited works that are as close as possible to your mixed methods study.

Mixed Methods Deficiencies in the Literature

In the next section, talk about what is missing in the literature that would help address the problem. Perhaps the missing part relates to the participants (studies are needed on Hispanics), or perhaps the relationship between variables is not well explained (results have been inconclusive about factors that dispose people to engage in cancer screening). It is in this section that mixed methods has an *important role.* The basic idea behind mixed methods is that something is gained when you (a) collect both quantitative and qualitative data and (b) integrate or use the databases in tandem. So, a deficiency in the literature may be directly related to a rationale for mixed methods. We may not have instruments that are culturally sensitive, and we may need to first explore before we begin measuring and gathering information (i.e., an exploratory sequential design). We may not have good measures for a construct or variables, and we may need to add interviews to ask participants about the construct so that we can get a "second opinion" on the construct (i.e., a convergent design). We may need to conduct research to learn how best to recruit participants into an intervention trial and begin our trial with qualitative focus groups (i.e., an intervention design).

The Audience

Identify the audience by determining which individuals will profit from the research study. Hopefully, every reader will be part of this audience, if you cast the net widely enough. You might think about the audience in terms of groups of people. How would policymakers, leaders, other researchers, practitioners in organizations or schools, or web audiences profit from the research? In this passage it is helpful to identify several audiences and be specific about how they might be helped by research that addresses the problem.

❖ WRITING A MIXED METHODS PURPOSE STATEMENT

This statement is the most important statement in a research project. It sets forth the aim or the central objective of the entire study. Without clarity in this statement, the reader will be lost throughout the project. What adds a challenge to writing this statement is that mixed methods is complex, with many moving parts. Readers need to encounter these parts early in a study—in the purpose statement or study aims section.

> A purpose statement establishes the major intent or objective of the study. It is the most important statement in a research project.

"Best Practices" Study Aims

In 2011, a study group developed the "Best Practices for Mixed Methods in the Health Sciences." This group was commissioned by the Office of Behavioral and Social Sciences Research at the National Institutes of Health (NIH). The product of this work group was the development of practices for mixed methods that might be used by those applying for NIH funds as well as those reviewing applications for funding. One section of this report (which is up on a website) addresses recommended study aims for an NIH project. It was felt that the study aims in a mixed methods project should include quantitative, qualitative, and mixed methods aims, and that these aims should relate to the type of mixed methods design being used. Moreover, and perhaps most importantly, the order of the "parts" of a study aim were discussed, and clearly members of the study group wanted to see a flow from the content topic (i.e., the topic being studied) to the methods (i.e., the procedures being used to study the topic). In other words, the methods were to take second position in the study aims, thus emphasizing the content over the methods. For example:

> The acceptance of the treatment procedures for AIDS/HIV (content) will be explored through the use of one-on-one interviews (methods).

A Sample Script

This thinking—that the content should be emphasized first—has played into the development of a mixed methods script that researchers might use to convey the purpose statement or study aim of a project. Purpose statements in mixed methods research are generally long and comprehensive. There are four parts of a good script for a mixed methods purpose statement:

1. *Intent.* Convey the general intent of the study. What do you hope to have accomplished by the end of the project? Keep this to one concise sentence.

2. *Design.* Next, mention the specific mixed methods design that you will use in your study (e.g., intervention design). Give a brief definition of this design and then mention the types of quantitative and qualitative data that you will collect and how the two databases will be integrated or combined.

3. *Data.* Next describe data collection procedures, including theories to be tested, individuals to be studied, variables to be analyzed, and central phenomena to be examined. For example, for a convergent design, you might say:

   In this study, [quantitative data] will be used to test the theory of [the theory] that predicts that [independent variables] will [positively, negatively] influence the [dependent variables] for [participants] at [the site]. The [type of qualitative data] will explore [the central phenomenon] for [participants] at [the site].

4. *Rationale.* End the purpose statement with the rationale that you are using for collecting both quantitative and qualitative data. Are you including qualitative data to help explain the quantitative results (i.e., explanatory sequential design)? Are you hoping to develop a more complete understanding of the problem (i.e., convergent design)? Is the rationale to have a better instrument (i.e., exploratory sequential design)?

Here is an example of an explanatory sequential design script. The researcher inserts information into the appropriate blanks:

This study will address [content aim]. An explanatory sequential mixed methods design will be used, and it will involve collecting quantitative data first and then explaining the quantitative results with in-depth qualitative data. In the first, quantitative phase of the study, [quantitative instrument] data will be collected from [participants] at [research site] to test [name of theory] to assess whether [independent variables] relate to [dependent variables]. The second, qualitative phase will be conducted as a follow-up to the quantitative results to help explain the quantitative results. In this exploratory follow-up, the tentative plan is to explore [the central phenomenon] with [participants] at [research site].

WRITING MIXED METHODS ❖ RESEARCH QUESTIONS

Since mixed methods is neither entirely quantitative nor entirely qualitative research but is something in between, how should the research questions be written for a mixed methods project? First, it is important to acknowledge that in published journal articles reporting mixed methods research, purpose statements (or study aims) and research questions are typically not both reported. More often than not, only purpose statements are reported. For graduate theses and dissertations in which the student needs to demonstrate his or her mastery of research, one often finds both a purpose statement and a research question. Proposals for funding also typically have both a purpose statement and a research question.

The role of research questions or hypotheses is to narrow down the purpose statement to questions or statements that will be specifically addressed in a project. In a mixed methods investigation, it is useful to have three types of questions:

1. Quantitative hypotheses or questions

2. Qualitative questions

3. **Mixed methods research questions**

Quantitative Hypotheses or Questions

Hypotheses are predictions of outcomes based on the literature or on theories. They can be stated in a null form ("There is no significance between . . .") or in a directional form ("Higher motivation leads to higher achievement"). Hypotheses are a formal way of writing questions, and they are typically found in the experimental research components of a mixed methods study. An alternative to constructing hypotheses would be to state research questions ("Is higher motivation related to higher achievement?"). Today, many mixed methods projects use research questions rather than hypotheses.

There are some fundamental guidelines in writing quantitative hypotheses or questions. First, you need to identify your variables, typically the major independent variables that influence your dependent variables or outcomes in a study. Variables are what you are measuring. In quantitative research, one typically either compares groups (in regard to the independent variable) or relates variables ("What factors contribute to low self-esteem?").

Second, the most rigorous quantitative studies base their hypotheses or questions on a theory that explains or predicts the relationship between the independent and dependent variables. Third, researchers need to select either hypotheses or research questions; typically, both are not used in a single mixed methods study. Fourth, be clear about the variables and their intent. The two most important variables are the independent and dependent variables—probably indicating cause and effect. Following these are other variables such as mediating variables (those that stand between the independent variable and the dependent variable as a means of influence), moderating variables (which combine with the independent variable to influence the outcome; e.g., age × motivation influences achievement); and covariates that are controlled in a study for their impact, such as demographics like social economic status, years of education, gender, and so forth. Fifth, to assist readers, it is helpful to make the word order of variables—from independent to dependent—consistent in each research question or hypothesis. Here is an example of parallel word order:

Does home resident location influence choice of a medical clinic?

Does input from family members influence the choice of a medical clinic?

Qualitative Research Questions

Good qualitative research questions also need to be written for a mixed methods project. In qualitative research, the investigator uses research questions rather than hypotheses. The form for these questions involves a central question followed by subquestions. The central question is the most general question that could be asked about a phenomenon. It typically begins with the words *how* or *what* (instead of *why*, which is typically associated with quantitative research). It also focuses on a central phenomenon or idea that the researcher wishes to explore (e.g., "What does it mean to wait for a kidney transplant?").

When phrasing the qualitative question, the researcher also uses action-oriented exploratory verbs, such as *discover, understand, describe,* or *report.* These questions often change during data collection as the researcher learns how to best collect data in the field. Using a specific type of qualitative design may influence the wording of the question as well. A grounded theory question might be, "What theory explains why people feel isolated in large organizations?" whereas a narrative research question might be, "What stories of survival do tsunami victims have?"

Mixed Methods Questions

This leads to the mixed methods question—a question that is new to most researches and not found to date in research methods textbooks. My colleagues and I developed this question because a question was being asked in mixed methods that was beyond the quantitative or qualitative questions. That "something beyond" can be represented by the intent of the mixed methods design. What additional information is being sought by having a design that integrates both the quantitative and qualitative research results? Knowing your mixed methods design will enable you to think about and pose the research question that the design is intended to answer. The following list represents typical mixed methods questions that relate to each of the six types of designs (basic and advanced):

Convergent

- To what extent do the qualitative results confirm the quantitative results?

Explanatory

- How do the qualitative data explain the quantitative results?

Exploratory

- To what extent do the qualitative findings generalize to a specified population?

Intervention

- How do the qualitative findings enhance the interpretation of the experimental outcomes?

Social Justice

- How do the qualitative findings enhance understanding of the quantitative results and lead to identification of inequalities?

Multistage

- A combination of the previous questions for the different phases in the project to address the overall research goal.

As you look over these mixed methods questions, you will see that they are stated in the form of research methods with a focus on data analysis results, both quantitative and qualitative. In other words, these mixed methods questions can be written from a "methods" orientation. Alternatively, they can be stated from more of a content-focused perspective, as in "How do the views of adolescent boys support their perspectives on self-esteem during their middle school years?" In this example, the "views" signify the qualitative portion of the study and "perspectives on self-esteem" signify the quantitative portion.

Finally, probably the best possible mixed methods question is one in which both the methods and the content are featured. This is called a "hybrid" mixed methods question, and again, it needs to reflect the type of design being used. An example is:

What results emerge from comparing the exploratory qualitative data about the self-esteem of boys with outcome quantitative instrument data measured on a self-esteem instrument?

In this example, we can easily determine the types of data being collected (qualitative data, instrument data) as well as perceive a focus on the content results of the study (self-esteem as measured by an instrument and during interviews).

❖ RECOMMENDATIONS FROM THIS CHAPTER

The approach taken in this chapter has been to emphasize an ideal structure for the introduction to a mixed methods study. A template has been given to outline the sections of the introduction, which should essentially identify the problem the study will address and surround it with a rationale. Most importantly, when citing the deficiencies in the existing literature, mention aspects missing from the methods orientation of previous studies. Consider your rationale for gathering both quantitative and qualitative data, and advance this mixed methods rationale as a solution to the deficiency in the past literature. A script should also help you craft a complete mixed methods purpose statement (or study aim). This script emphasizes the intent of the study, the mixed methods design used, the forms of data collection employed, and the reason for combining both forms of data. Finally, in writing a good mixed methods study, include quantitative questions or hypotheses, qualitative questions, and a mixed methods question. The order of the questions should follow the type of mixed methods design being used (e.g., start with qualitative questions in an exploratory sequential design). Also, the mixed methods question should indicate what the researcher hopes to learn from his or her mixed methods design, and it can be stated in a methods way, a content way, or as some combination of the two.

ADDITIONAL READINGS ❖

Creswell, J. W., & Plano Clark, V. L. (2011). *Designing and conducting mixed methods research* (2nd ed.). Thousand Oaks, CA: SAGE.

Maxwell, J. A. (2013). *Qualitative research design: An interactive approach* (3rd ed.). Thousand Oaks, CA: SAGE.

For more information on developing research questions, see:

Plano Clark, V. L., & Badiee, M. (2010). Research questions in mixed methods research. In A. Tashakkori & C. Teddlie (Eds.), *SAGE handbook of mixed methods in social and behavioral research* (2nd ed., pp. 275–304). Thousand Oaks, CA: SAGE.

CHAPTER 7

SAMPLING AND INTEGRATION ISSUES

❖ TOPICS IN THE CHAPTER

- Sampling for both the quantitative and qualitative strands of the mixed methods study
- How sampling issues differ by type of design
- Types of integration in a mixed methods study
- Representing integration through a joint display

❖ THE ISSUES OF SAMPLING AND INTEGRATION

In Chapter 4, I introduced some of the challenges that need to be anticipated when conducting the three basic designs and the three advanced designs. These challenges, which I have referred to as "methodological issues" or "validity issues" in conducting mixed methods research, sometimes relate to how a researcher bridges from one dataset to another, incorporates a lens or framework into a study, or develops an instrument for measurement that has good psychometric properties. A close inspection of these challenges, however, shows that the major issues confronting the mixed methods researcher relate to the two issues of sampling and integration. **Sampling in mixed methods research** refers to the procedures for selecting participants (and sites) in both quantitative and qualitative research and to the sampling strategies employed within each of the designs. Questions of size and the nature of participants fill the pages of mixed methods writings. **Integration**, on the other hand, refers to how one brings together the qualitative and quantitative results in a mixed methods study, and how this combination relates to the type of design used. Both issues have been contested and debated within the mixed methods literature, and authors such as Bryman (2006) suggest that most studies alleging to be mixed methods do not illustrate an integration of the two databases. Instead, researchers tend to keep them separate. Thus, both sampling and integration deserve attention in our mixed methods projects.

> **Integration** refers to how one brings together the qualitative and quantitative results in a mixed methods study. The way the researcher combines the data needs to relate to the type of mixed methods design used.

SAMPLING

There are several sampling issues that play into designing and conducting a good mixed methods research study. At the outset, the sampling for both the qualitative and quantitative samples needs to follow rigorous procedures. This means attending to sample size, identifying the participants in the sample, and considering what questions to ask them through instruments or through more open-ended procedures such as interviews. Then, as the design unfolds, the sampling *within* the design needs to be logical and rigorous.

> **Sampling Issues to Consider**
>
> • The use of rigorous procedures in both qualitative and quantitative strands
> • The sample size

Quantitative Sampling

Recruiting individuals to the sample needs to be done carefully so that the right participants enter the study. Permissions then need to be obtained from these individuals, following institutional review board (IRB) procedures. Permissions may also be needed from key personnel at the research sites being studied (e.g., administrators at the hospital, principals at the school). Attention also needs to be given to selecting the appropriate sampling strategy. As mentioned in Chapter 3, a good sampling strategy is **random sampling**, but this approach may not be available, given the need to sample individuals who are available or who volunteer. Sampling may fall into the category of probability sampling, such as in simple random sampling, stratified sampling, or multistage cluster sampling. It can also consist of nonprobability sampling, as in convenience or snowball sampling (where people recommend others for inclusion in the study) (Creswell, 2012).

Sample size is another consideration. It is important to select as large a sample as possible, because with a large sample there is less room for error in how well the sample reflects the characteristics of the population. Fortunately, in both survey research and experimental research, there are aids to help you select an appropriate sample size. In survey research, I would suggest that you use a sampling error formula discussed in a book such as *Survey Research Methods* (Fowler, 2008). Tables in this book will indicate the appropriate calculation for determining size of a sample based on the chance (proportion) that the sample will be evenly divided on a question, sampling error, and a confidence interval. To estimate sample size for an experiment, this formula takes into consideration the level of statistical significance (alpha), the amount of power desired in a study (e.g., 0.80, 0.90, 0.95), and the effect size (the practical difference you are willing to live with). From this formula, you can determine an appropriate size for the groups in your experiment. For experiments, I suggest that you examine books on power analysis, such as *Design Sensitivity* (Lipsey, 1990).

In quantitative sampling, use a formula to determine the desired sample size. Conduct a power analysis when carrying out experiments.

Qualitative Sampling

Whereas the intent of quantitative sampling is to be able to generalize from a sample to a population, the intent of qualitative research is quite different. Qualitative research sampling is simply the purposeful selection of a sample of participants who can best help you understand the central phenomenon that you are exploring. This is far from an "anything goes" type of sampling.

A number of purposeful sampling strategies exist, such as maximal variation sampling, in which individuals who differ are selected so that diverse perspectives—a goal of good qualitative research—are built into the design; or critical sampling, in which specific individual cases or criteria are used to select individuals to further learn about how they are experiencing the phenomenon. Additional forms of purposeful sampling, before the study begins and after the study has commenced (e.g., snowball sampling, confirming/disconfirming sampling), are available (see Creswell, 2012). As with quantitative sampling, individual participants in a qualitative study need to be recruited for participation and permissions need to be granted at several levels (e.g., IRB approval, site approval, individual participant approval).

Sample size in qualitative research has been a topic of debate for many years. The traditional stance on size is not to specify a size but to consider size as a function of when **saturation** occurs in a study. Saturation can be defined as the point in data collection when the researcher gathers data from several participants and the collection of data from *new* participants does not add substantially to the codes or themes being developed. At this point, the researcher ceases collecting data. Another method of determining sample size—and this is one I endorse—is to examine a number of published qualitative studies by design (e.g., narrative research, phenomenology, grounded theory, ethnography, case study research) and use the sample sizes being reported in the articles. Alternatively, suggestions for sample sizes might be sought from research methods books covering the design used. I have recommended using one or two individuals for a narrative study, 3 to 10 participants for a phenomenology, 20 to 30 subjects for a grounded theory study, a single culture-sharing group for ethnography, and four to five cases for case study research (Creswell, 2013); for each of these numbers, specific published studies can be cited to back up my numbers.

> In qualitative sampling, purposefully select participants who can best help you understand the central phenomenon that you are exploring.

Mixed Methods Sampling

It is helpful to consider how sampling proceeds within each of the major designs. In a *convergent design*, as shown in Figure 7.1, the question of sampling arises in terms of collecting both quantitative and qualitative data.

Figure 7.1 Sampling in a Convergent Design

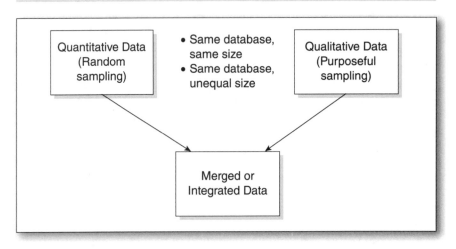

In this design, the quantitative sample proceeds from a random or nonrandom sampling procedure, while the qualitative sample proceeds from purposeful sampling. Two issues arise in the selection of samples for these two databases: Should the participants come from the same population? Should both samples be of equal size? The answer to the first question is yes, the participants should ideally come from the same population. In some cases, mixed methods researchers use a different unit of analysis for each sample (e.g., hospital administrators for the quantitative sample and health providers for the qualitative sample). Having different units of analysis should work especially well when the intent of the convergent design is to compare different perspectives. If the intent is to validate one database with the other, then I would recommend using the same individuals.

The answer to the second question is less clear. In qualitative research, a small sample is studied in order to build individual perspectives; in quantitative research, a large sample is collected so that the results can be generalized from the sample to a population. For both the quantitative and the qualitative strand, we need to consider sample size options. One option found in the literature is to have the same sample size for both quantitative and qualitative data collection. This procedure, of course, leads to a large qualitative sample that costs time and resources. Another option is to weigh the qualitative data so that the cases are equivalent to the quantitative cases. This technique entails essentially adopting a quantitative perspective toward the data, and raises the issue of how the qualitative cases might be weighted to be equivalent to the number of quantitative cases. A final approach is to accept the differences in sampling between the quantitative sample and the qualitative sample. Qualitative researchers might well argue that equal size is unnecessary because the data tell different stories (i.e., general trends on the quantitative side and detailed perspectives on the qualitative side). I have seen convergent designs that embrace each of these possibilities, so I will leave it up to you to decide which option to select.

In an *explanatory sequential design*, the random sampling proceeds on the quantitative strand and the purposeful sampling on the qualitative strand. As shown in Figure 7.2, issues arise as to whether the qualitative sample needs to be drawn from the quantitative sample and whether the sizes of the two samples should be the same or different. Clearly, if the intent of the design is for the qualitative data to explain the quantitative results, the individuals in the qualitative sample need to be drawn from the pool of participants in the quantitative sample. Therefore, the qualitative sample is a subset of the quantitative sample, and because qualitative data collection consists of obtaining information from fewer participants than the quantitative sample, the sizes of the two samples will be unequal. One popular technique for identifying the participants for the qualitative follow-up sample is to ask for volunteers when collecting quantitative data on instruments. Also, in the explanatory sequential design, the results from the quantitative strand

Figure 7.2 Sampling in an Explanatory Sequential Design

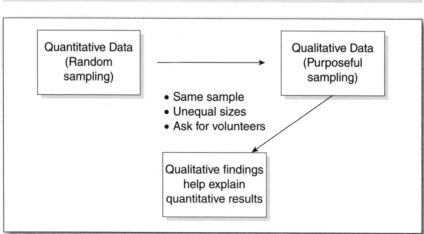

help inform the questions asked in the qualitative sample, and so participants from the qualitative sample need to be individuals who are capable of answering the qualitative questions.

In an *exploratory sequential design*, the approach to sampling is opposite the one taken in the explanatory sequential design. As shown in Figure 7.3, the sample for the quantitative follow-up may be different from the sample for the initial qualitative strand of the study. The qualitative data collection needs to be purposeful and the quantitative sample as randomly selected as possible. However, because the first phase is exploratory, the sample drawn is based on a small number of individuals intentionally selected to help explore the problem. An intermediate phase then uses the data results from the exploratory phase to develop something quantitative—typically a new or modified instrument, new measures, or new intervention procedures. Then the quantitative element developed is tested with a large sample. If the quantitative test in the final phase is intended to determine whether the qualitative themes in the first phase can be generalized to a large sample, then, yes, the two data collections need to be from the same sample, or at least the same population. But

Figure 7.3 Sampling in an Exploratory Sequential Design

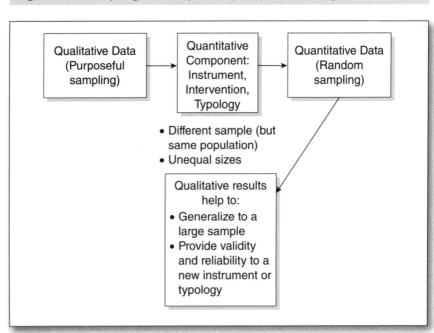

if the intent of the design is to develop a new or modified instrument, set of variables, or intervention procedures, then the requirement that the two data collections come from the same sample or population may be somewhat relaxed. So the two samples may be different, not only in size but also in terms of their population membership. That is, the samples are ideally from the same population, but this is not absolutely necessary. In terms of size, the two samples will not be equal. The sample can differ between the first and the final phase of an exploratory sequential design.

For advanced designs, the sampling procedures will follow the basic design procedures, because these basic designs are a centerpiece within the advanced designs. It might be helpful, however, to examine the sampling in an intervention design as an example of one advanced design. As shown in Figure 7.4, we still see purposeful sampling in the qualitative components brought into the experiment and quantitative sampling (i.e., random assignment) in the experimental part of the study. It is the qualitative sampling in this design that needs to be given some thought. If qualitative data are collected prior to the experiment, then the intent must be made clear, and it needs to be provided in the way that is most useful for the experiment. For example, if the intent is to gather qualitative data *before* the experiment in order to best recruit participants to the experiment, sampling needs to intentionally focus on the participants sought for the experiment, and the

Figure 7.4 Sampling in an Intervention Design

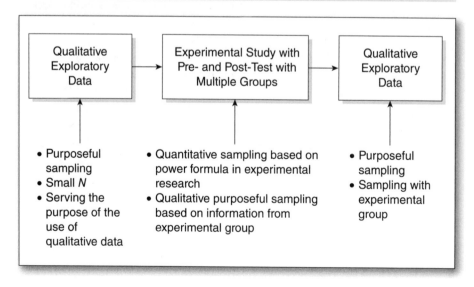

questions should be phrased to contribute to this intent. If qualitative data are collected *during* the experiment, the question arises as to whether the sample will be the individuals in the control group, those in the experimental group, or both. Typically, in intervention designs, mixed methods researchers collect qualitative data from the experimental group only, probably because of resource limitations and also because they want to learn how the experimental group is experiencing the treatment. If qualitative data are collected *after* the experiment to follow up on the outcome results, again, normally the experimental group is sampled because it is the group that received the treatment.

Mixed methods sampling procedures should follow the particular mixed methods design. The researcher needs to be aware of design-specific issues.

❖ INTEGRATION

How sampling is carried out, then, relates to how it is used within specific designs. The same is true of integration. Integration is the place in the mixed methods research process where the quantitative and the qualitative phases intersect (or bump up against each other). Morse and Niehaus (2009) call this the point of interface, and their diagrams contain arrows pointing to this interface to make it explicit within a design. *Integration* might be seen as an alternative term for *mixing* in mixed methods research. If you were to look up the dictionary definition of *mixing*, you would find that it means that one thing actually dissolves into the other or that one thing connects to another. For example, in cake batter, the flour dissolves into the mixture. When we add raisins into the cake, they remain intact, but they are still "mixed" into the batter. The same is true with mixed methods: The quantitative data and the qualitative data can either dissolve into each other or remain separate.

Types of Integration

Integration can be found in several possible places in a mixed methods study (i.e., the arrow can be placed in many possible locations) (see Fetters, Curry, & Creswell, 2013). It can be found in the data collection phase, where the researcher might collect survey data that contain both closed-ended responses and open-ended responses. It can be found in the data analysis phase, where the researcher might gather quantitative data, analyze it, and report the qualitative data and results that help explain the quantitative findings. It can be found in experiments, where the researcher might collect qualitative data after the experiment concludes and report the results, first the experimental outcomes and then the qualitative follow-up results. It can be found in the discussion section of the study, in which the researcher might compare the qualitative results with the quantitative results. Finally, it can be found in tables or graphs, in which the investigator might array the quantitative results against the qualitative results.

Possible Locations of Integration in a Study

- Data collection
- Data analysis
- Results section of experiments

Four types of integration of quantitative and qualitative data exist:

- Merging of the data, which occurs when the results of the analyses of quantitative and quantitative data are brought together and compared. This merging is found in a convergent design.
- Explanation of the data, which occurs when qualitative data are used to explain the results of the quantitative data. This explaining is seen in an explanatory sequential design.
- Building of the data, which occurs when the qualitative data results are used to build a quantitative phase in a study, such as creation of a new instrument, discovery of new variables, or generation of new intervention features. This building occurs in an exploratory sequential design.
- Embedding of the data, which occurs when qualitative data are used to augment or support the quantitative data, such as when qualitative data are added into an experiment. This embedding or nesting is found in an intervention design.

A graphic can best capture these different types of integration, as shown in Figure 7.5.

Figure 7.5 Types of Integration in Mixed Methods Research

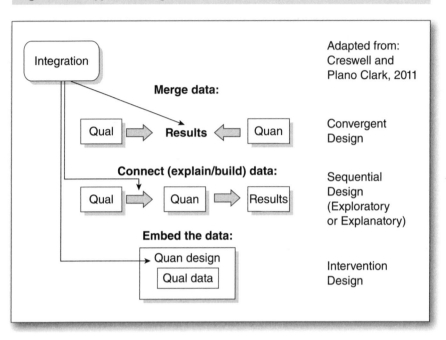

How Integration Is Represented in a Mixed Methods Study

The mixed methods researcher has various ways in which to represent integration in a study. It can appear as a passage in the data collection, in a results passage in data analysis, or in a discussion or conclusion section at the end of a study. In a larger sense, integration can be the skills brought by different researchers to a mixed methods team or the use of multiple philosophical perspectives to guide an inquiry.

A popular way to represent integration is through a discussion in which the quantitative and qualitative results are arrayed one after the other, in parallel fashion. In this approach, the researcher discusses first the quantitative results and then the qualitative results and indicates how these two results compare. An alternative would be to start with the qualitative results and follow with the quantitative results. This model is popular for use with the convergent design.

Another approach is to develop a table or graph that illustrates the results from both databases. This table or graph is called a **joint display**.

A joint display arrays the results together in a table or graph so that the reader can easily compare the two results. Several options exist for how this joint display might be composed.

- A *side-by-side joint display* table would array both qualitative themes and quantitative statistical results side by side in a table. In addition, one final column in the table would discuss the differences and similarities between the themes and the statistical results. This type of display is often used in a convergent design. From this table a reader would be able to understand how the qualitative and the quantitative results converge or diverge.
- A *theme-by-statistics joint display* is another option. In this display, the qualitative themes are arrayed on the horizontal axis while the quantitative data are presented on the vertical axis. Within the cells, one can find quotes, frequency counts, or both. This display is typically used in a convergent design. The statistical results may be presented by categories (e.g., type of provider, such as medical assistant, doctor, or nurse) or on a continuous scale (e.g., level of agreement, from "strongly agree" to "strongly disagree"). From this table, a reader would be able to assess how the themes differ from the numeric data by examining the information in the cells.
- A *follow-up results joint display* is used in an explanatory sequential design. This type of display, as shown in Table 7.1, presents the quantitative results in one column, the qualitative follow-up results in a second column, and information about how the qualitative findings help to explain the quantitative results in a final column. From this table, a reader would be able to determine how the qualitative data help to explain the quantitative results.
- A *building into a quantitative instrument or measure display* helps to illustrate the integration of an exploratory qualitative phase with a quantitative instrument or measurement phase. In an exploratory sequential design, one of the challenges is how to use the qualitative data for building new measures or instruments. In this type of joint display, the researcher could present the exploratory qualitative findings in the first column, the measures or variables derived from the qualitative findings in the second column, and how the measures and variables formed new scales or instruments in the final column. In this way a reader would understand how the qualitative initial phase was used to build into a quantitative phase. A variation on this table would be to array in one column the categories of quotes, codes, and

Table 7.1 Integration in a Joint Display for an Explanatory Sequential Design

Quantitative Results	Qualitative Follow-Up Interviews Explaining Quantitative Results	How Qualitative Findings Helped to Explain Quantitative Results
The more experienced the teachers, and the greater the use of the program materials, the higher the student scores.	Themes: More experienced teachers were willing to use the materials. More experienced teachers were able to blend the materials into their own approach. More experienced teachers were more willing to follow the school's approach	Motivation and willingness surfaced as explanations. How the teachers blended the materials was highlighted in the explanations.

themes, and to position in the next column examples of elements in an instrument, such as items (converted from quotes), variables (converted from codes), and scales (converted from themes).

These are a few examples of ways to represent integration of the quantitative and qualitative results in joint displays that are beginning to appear in published mixed methods studies. Other examples include information presented in a graph (e.g., geographical information system graphs of regions differing on certain quantitative variables and qualitative quotes or themes attached to the regions), joint displays organized by participants or cases, and displays that show the transformation of qualitative data into quantitative counts.

❖ RECOMMENDATIONS FROM THIS CHAPTER

In this chapter you have learned about the issues of sampling and integration in mixed methods studies. When designing your sampling in a mixed methods study, I recommend that you make it rigorous on both the quantitative and the qualitative side. Also, sampling procedures need to be considered with respect to each type of mixed methods design. Integration is another central point in a mixed methods study. It can be included in the data collection, data analysis, and discussion or conclusion sections of a project. I recommend that you identify the method of integration as merging, explaining, building, or embedding; and represent the integration through joint displays that array the qualitative and quantitative results together in tables or graphs.

ADDITIONAL READINGS

Bryman, A. (2006). Integrating quantitative and qualitative research: How is it done? *Qualitative Research, 6,* 97–113. doi: 10.1177/1468794106058877

Creswell, J. W. (2012). *Educational research: Planning, conducting, and evaluating quantitative and qualitative research.* Boston, MA: Pearson.

Fetters, M. D., Curry, L. A., & Creswell, J. W. (2013). Achieving integration in mixed methods designs: Principles and practices. *Health Services Research, 48,* 2134–2156. doi: 10.1111/1475-6773.12117

Fowler, F. J., Jr. (2008). *Survey research methods* (4th ed.). Thousand Oaks, CA: SAGE.

Guetterman, T., Creswell, J. W., & Kuckartz, U. (in press). Using visual displays in mixed methods research. In M. McCrudden, G. Schraw, and C. Buckendahl (Eds.), *Use of visual displays in research and testing: Coding, interpreting, and reporting data.* Charlotte, NC: Information Age Publishing.

Lipsey, M. W. (1990). *Design sensitivity: Statistical power for experimental research.* Newbury Park, CA: SAGE.

CHAPTER 8

WRITING A MIXED METHODS STUDY FOR PUBLICATION

❖ TOPICS IN THE CHAPTER

- Suitable journals for mixed methods publications
- Criteria for evaluating mixed methods articles for publication
- Types of mixed methods publications
- General considerations for writing
- Writing structure and type of design

❖ LOCATING A SUITABLE JOURNAL

We all know that mixed methods articles tend to be long because of the necessity of including quantitative data collection and analysis as well as qualitative data collection and analysis. Further, the integration of the two databases requires space as well. Most scholarly journals simply do not have space for long studies. Complicating this issue is the need to educate readers about mixed methods.

As authors know, finding the right journal for mixed methods is critically important. The empirical study must fit the topics included in and the approach used by the journal. Since mixed methods is a relatively new methodology, authors often write and ask about what journals they should submit their study to. There are three general classes of journals that may publish a mixed methods study:

1. There are journals that publish only mixed methods research. This list is continually growing, but I would put on this list at the moment:

   a. *Journal of Mixed Methods Research*
   b. *International Journal of Multiple Research Approaches (online journal)*
   c. *Field Methods*
   d. *Quality and Quantity*

2. Other journals are friendly to mixed methods and often publish mixed methods studies:

   a. *International Journal of Social Research Methodology*
   b. *Qualitative Inquiry*
   c. *Qualitative Research*
   d. *British Medical Journal (BMJ)*

3. In the final category I would put journals that have published mixed methods studies. This list is growing, and here I can include only a few examples:

   a. *Annals of Family Medicine*
   b. *American Educational Research Journal*
   c. *Circulation*

CRITERIA USED TO ❖ EVALUATE *JMMR* ARTICLES

I cofounded the *Journal of Mixed Methods Research* in 2007. Over the space of about four years, I reviewed close to 300 different mixed methods studies submitted to the journal. Over time, I began to look for certain features that I wanted to see in all mixed methods empirical articles. When a mixed methods manuscript came in, here is how I determined whether it was a mixed methods investigation worthy of sending out for review:

- I first looked at the methods section to see if the study contained both qualitative and quantitative data.
- I then looked throughout the article to see if the authors actually "integrated," or combined, the two databases. In a good mixed methods study, the databases are integrated. I will admit that sometimes it was difficult to determine how and in what way the authors actually "integrated" the two databases. A look at the results and discussion sections often helped to locate this aspect of the studies.
- Next, I looked for whether the author or authors were familiar with the mixed methods literature and actually cited recent mixed methods books.
- Last, I was curious about the mixed methods features that the authors had embedded in the study. For instance, did they state a rationale for why they were using and integrating both quantitative and qualitative data? Did they mention "mixed methods" in the title? Did they have features such as mixed methods questions or joint displays? Was the study more of a methodological article or an empirical study that used mixed methods? These additional features set off a study as a rigorous mixed methods project.

❖ TWO TYPES OF MIXED METHODS ARTICLES

When my colleagues and I designed the content for the *Journal of Mixed Methods Research*, we envisioned two types of manuscripts that might come in: empirical studies using mixed methods research and methodological articles discussing how to conduct mixed methods research. Both types indeed came in.

Methodological Articles

From the methodological (or theoretical) articles, we can learn how to conduct mixed methods research, whether these articles discuss strategies for validation (Leech, Dellinger, Brannagan, & Tanaka, 2009), how to publish mixed methods research (Stange, Crabtree, & Miller, 2006), or how to apply mixed methods to specific fields, such as health disparities (Stewart, Makwarimba, Barnfather, Letourneau, & Neufeld, 2008) or palliative care (Farquhar, Ewing, & Booth, 2011). There does seem to be a structure to these methodological articles, and they often begin with an overview of mixed methods research (e.g., Farquhar et al., 2011; Stewart, et al., 2008). This overview may answer the following questions:

- What is mixed methods?
- Why is the term *mixed methods* used as a label for this methodology?
- What are the key assumptions behind using mixed methods?
- Why should we use mixed methods?
- How should we use mixed methods (e.g., designs)?
- What is the value added by mixed methods (e.g., benefits)?
- What are some challenges in using mixed methods?

Empirical Articles

An empirical study in mixed methods is a research investigation in which the author studies a content area (or disease area) and uses mixed methods research as the methodology for the study. The writing for this type of study, when submitted to a journal, needs to be solid in advancing new knowledge about the content area, but it also should consider several mixed methods research components.

Mixed methods studies tend to be long and include many pages of text, because it takes space to report the research components of two types of data collection and two types of data analysis as well as to discuss integration of the two forms of data. Some journals have a restricted word length of 3,000 words or possibly 6,000 words—quite short for a mixed methods article. Other journals allow more space. For example, the *Journal of Mixed Methods Research* allows articles with 8,000 to 10,000 words.

When length is a problem, the question becomes how to shorten the study. One way to think about this is by closely studying a series of articles: one sent in as a quantitative article, one sent in as a qualitative article, and a third sent in as a mixed methods article. My colleagues and I have done some research using this approach, and we asked students in one of our classes to look at three studies from the same project and ask themselves what the authors shortened for the "overall" mixed methods journal article. We learned that the third type, the overall mixed methods article, typically had a shortened methods discussion for both the quantitative and qualitative aspects. The authors also organized the results around either the quantitative results or the qualitative results in the "overall" article, thus avoiding the need to present all of the quantitative and qualitative results. Finally, the authors used tables to condense information so that less space was taken up in discussions. These are all useful strategies for reducing a large mixed methods article into a shorter, more manageable article for journals with reduced word limits.

As is evident in the example just given, a helpful way to think about writing empirical articles for mixed methods research is to think about generating three written products from a single study: a quantitative article, a qualitative article, and an overall mixed methods article. These articles could go out to different journals. The sequence of submission could be the quantitative and qualitative articles first, followed by the mixed methods article. When this approach is used, authors need to provide a cross-reference or "crosswalk" from one publication to the others so that readers see all three articles as belonging to one mixed methods investigation. A fourth type of article, a methodological article discussing the unique mixed methods procedures used in a study, could be added to the set of three articles from a research project.

Few studies have addressed how to publish mixed methods research, but an exception would be the article by Stange et al. (2006) on publishing a multi-method study. They recommend five strategies that are popular in primary (health) care:

- Publish quantitative and qualitative studies separately, but cross-reference the articles.
- Publish concurrent or sequential quantitative and qualitative papers in the same journal. A few journals will permit this multiple-paper approach.
- Publish an "integrated" article but place additional details in an appendix or online resource site. I consider this article the "overall" mixed methods study, and it can be shortened by placing methods details elsewhere.
- Publish separate qualitative and quantitative papers, and then publish a third paper focused on "overarching lessons." This last article will be an "overall" mixed methods study that is longer and includes a detailed methods section.
- Publish your results in an online discussion. This is an attractive format for long manuscripts. Journals that publish empirical research studies online are becoming more popular.

These are helpful suggestions for creating multiple manuscripts for publication from a single project, and they seem most relevant for large-scale, multi-year, funded projects involving many staff members when publishing outlets vary in their acceptance of word length.

Another consideration for writing a mixed methods empirical manuscript is educating readers about the nature of mixed methods research. This could be done in the methods section of a manuscript, but, at a minimum, readers need to know a definition of mixed methods research, the value of using it, and its potential use within the content area being addressed in the study. Many different "boilerplate" examples of the general topics that might be included exist in the literature. An example would be the Creswell and Zhang (2009) article, in which we discussed the origin of mixed methods (the appropriate term for the methodology), a definition of mixed methods, the core characteristics associated with mixed methods, the specific forms that integration has taken in the field, and popular mixed methods designs.

STRUCTURING THE EMPIRICAL ❖ ARTICLE TO REFLECT THE DESIGN

It should be quite noticeable that the structure of published empirical mixed methods studies varies from article to article. A close review of these structures, however, shows that the structure varies from one type of design to another. To examine the structure of mixed methods published studies, I suggest that you locate about 20 studies incorporating the design that you propose to use (e.g., a convergent design), look closely at the results and discussion sections, and study the flow of ideas. This analysis will produce, I believe, a picture of the structure for your specific design. I have done this, and the following discussion highlights the structures that I have found for the major types of mixed methods research designs. Two points are important:

1. The writing or composition structure needs to match the type of design and, more specifically, the order of the quantitative, qualitative, and integrative phases of the research design.

2. The mixed methods components can typically be found in the *methods*, *results*, and *discussion* sections of a manuscript. Thus, in the examples that follow, these sections will be italicized.

Convergent Design Structure

You will recall that a convergent design is one that merges the quantitative and qualitative databases in order to generate two interpretations of key common questions. Before the two databases are brought together, the researcher collects and analyzes each database separately. Therefore, in the *methods* section of a mixed methods publication on a study using a convergent design, one would have separate quantitative and qualitative *data collection* and *data analysis* sections. It does not make any difference whether quantitative or qualitative research comes first in these two sections; the idea is simply that they are separate. Results are reported for the analysis of each type of data separately in the *results* section of the report. Statistical results are reported, and the thematic qualitative results are reported. The integration of the two databases often appears in the *discussion* section of a manuscript. It is here that we see "side-by-side" comparisons. If the convergent design researchers have included joint displays, these may be found in the *results* section or the *discussion* section (along with other features, such as limitations of the study, the available literature, and directions for future research).

Explanatory Sequential Design Structure

You may recall that in an explanatory sequential design, the project begins with a quantitative phase, which is then followed by a qualitative phase that helps to explain the quantitative results. Thus, in a written manuscript using this design, the *methods* section should first cover the quantitative data (e.g., instruments) and then the qualitative data (e.g., interview procedures and questions). Next, the *results* section should include three parts: (a) the discussion about the quantitative statistical results, (b) the discussion about what elements of the quantitative results need to be further explained (e.g., significant results, nonsignificant results, outliers, demographics), and (c) the qualitative results that help to explain the quantitative results. The *discussion* section might then reinforce this order of ideas by summarizing the major elements in all three steps that reflect the flow of ideas in the design (as well as include other features, such as limitation of the study, the available literature, and directions for future research).

Exploratory Sequential Design Structure

An exploratory design, you may recall, starts with the qualitative, exploratory phase; builds into a second, quantitative phase, such as developing an instrument or creating materials for an intervention; and then has a third, quantitative phase of actually testing the instrument or materials with a large sample of a population. The writing structure for this type of design would include a *methods* section that presents the qualitative data collection and procedures followed by the quantitative data. The *results* section would first report on the qualitative findings, then describe the quantitative feature (e.g., instrument) developed out of the qualitative findings, and finally report on the quantitative results of testing out the feature (in short, it should have three sections). A *discussion* section would repeat, albeit briefly, the three sections found in the *results* (as well as other features, such as limitations of the study, the available literature, and directions for future research).

Intervention Design Structure

In an intervention mixed methods design, qualitative data is inserted into an experimental trial at different times, such as before the trial begins (e.g., to help design an intervention that will work), during the trial (e.g., to help create an understanding of the processes treatment participants experience), or after the trial (e.g., to help explain the quantitative outcomes using qualitative data collection and analysis). This design is considered an "advanced" mixed methods design because an extra feature (i.e., the intervention trial) is added to the basic design. In an intervention design, the *methods* section would include a discussion of the intervention trial (or experiment) followed by a discussion about the collection and analysis of the qualitative data. The *results* section would then include the outcome results of the trial as well as the qualitative themes. The order of presentation of these topics depends on how the qualitative data are used in the study—whether they come before the trial (i.e., the qualitative themes are mentioned first, followed by the experiment), during the trial (the qualitative data are integrated with the experimental results), or after the trial (the intervention results are reported first, followed by the qualitative findings). In the *discussion*, the writer then reviews the intervention results and the qualitative findings, and then adds information about how the qualitative findings provide additional insight into the intervention trial. (As mentioned, the *discussion* also includes other features, such as limitations of the study, the available literature, and directions for future research.)

CBPR Mixed Methods Design Structure

One use of an advanced design is incorporation of a theoretical orientation into the basic design. An excellent example of this theoretical orientation (or philosophical approach, or simply, social justice approach) can be found in community-based participatory research (CBPR) studies, in which CBPR becomes an overarching framework threading throughout the study. CBPR involves stakeholders in many aspects of a study. An ideal writing structure, then, would describe community involvement through stakeholders in each phase of the research in which they have been involved (e.g., in forming the research questions, in the data collection, and so forth). The *methods* section would discuss the points in the study in which the stakeholders were involved. The *results* would present information dependent on the basic design used in the project, and the *discussion* section would elaborate on how the stakeholders added additional insight into the project (as well as include other features, such as limitations of the study, the available literature, and directions for future research).

❖ A CHECKLIST OF ELEMENTS TO INCLUDE IN A PUBLICATION

I feel that it is helpful to have a checklist that manuscript writers might consider as they review their mixed methods empirical investigation for submission to a journal (see Table 8.1). This checklist would also be appropriate for individuals submitting a doctoral dissertation or master's thesis or an application for federal or foundation funding. The order of items on this checklist reflects the order in which they would appear in a published manuscript.

❖ RECOMMENDATIONS FROM THIS CHAPTER

We can learn much from studying examples of mixed methods studies and being curious about how they are written—especially in regard to the

Table 8.1 A Checklist of Elements to Include
in a Mixed Methods Manuscript Submission

- Include a mixed methods title
- Add an abstract that conveys the type of mixed methods design used
- Convey how the problem merits a mixed methods study (rationale)
- Create a mixed methods study aim or purpose statement
- Create quantitative, qualitative, and mixed methods research questions
- Consider stating the worldview underlying the research and the use of theory (social science, transformative)
- Include rigorous mixed methods components

  o Discuss the advantages of using mixed methods
  o Identify the type of mixed methods design used
  o Present a diagram of procedures
  o Identify methodological challenges
  o Describe quantitative and qualitative data collection and analysis
  o Discuss ethical issues
  o Discuss validity

- Report the results in a manner consistent with the mixed methods design
- Discuss the integration of quantitative and qualitative data

methods, the results, and the discussion. Attention needs to be given to the writing structure of a mixed methods study. The preferences of publication outlets, the criteria that experienced mixed methods researchers use to evaluate their studies, and the special requirements for journal articles (e.g., word length) also need our careful attention. A rigorous mixed methods study contains many mixed methods elements, and it is helpful to consult a checklist of these elements in writing for publication.

ADDITIONAL READINGS ❖

To locate information about journals for publication, see:

- Cabell's Directories of Publishing Opportunities (www.cabells.com/index.aspx)
- Ulrich's Web (www.ulrichsweb.com/ulrichsweb)
- The University of North Carolina at Charlotte's, 2011 list (http://guides.library.uncc.edu/coed_faculty)

For guidance on writing, see:

Creswell, J. W., & Plano Clark, V. L. (2011). *Designing and conducting mixed methods research* (2nd ed.). Thousand Oaks, CA: SAGE.

Dahlberg, B., Wittink, M. N., & Gallo, J. J. (2010). Funding and publishing integrated studies: Writing effective mixed methods manuscripts and grant proposals. In A. Tashakkori & C. Teddlie (Eds.), *SAGE handbook of mixed methods in social and behavioral research* (pp. 775–802). Thousand Oaks, CA: SAGE.

O'Cathain, A. (2009). Reporting mixed methods projects. In S. Andrew & E. J. Halcomb (Eds.), *Mixed methods research for nursing and the health sciences* (pp. 135–158). West Sussex, UK: Blackwell.

Sandelowski, M. (2003). Tables or tableaux? The challenges of writing and reading mixed methods studies. In A. Tashakkori & C. Teddlie (Eds.), *Handbook of mixed methods in social and behavioral research* (pp. 321–350). Thousand Oaks, CA: SAGE.

Stange, K. C., Crabtree, B. F., & Miller, W. L. (2006). Publishing multimethod research. *Annals of Family Medicine, 4,* 292–294. doi: 10.1370/afm.615

CHAPTER 9

EVALUATING THE QUALITY OF A MIXED METHODS STUDY

TOPICS IN THE CHAPTER

- Whether to use standards to evaluate mixed methods
- Standards used by the *Journal of Mixed Methods Research*
- Standards available in the literature
- "Best practices" recommendations of the National Institutes of Health (NIH)

HOW CRITERIA ARE BEING APPLIED ❖

As the field of mixed methods grows and matures, it is only natural for writers and scholars to begin to consider standards or guidelines for assessing the quality of mixed methods studies. A mature scientific field does have standards of quality that scholars use to assess projects and to evaluate a study. But also as a field matures, there is often disagreement about what constitutes quality and whether individuals from different disciplines and fields can agree on the quality characteristics. What has emerged to date in mixed methods has been a number of standards that individuals use—whether they are from journals or funding agencies or individual criteria that faculty and students might impose. Unquestionably, mixed methods is developing, and firm standards are not in place for assessing quality.

Different audiences are using standards of quality, whether they are being openly acknowledged or not. Journals typically include a page in their guidelines listing the criteria that reviewers use to assess the quality of a manuscript. Sometimes these guidelines are highly detailed; at other times, they are more abstract and general. In the mixed methods field, the journals to which authors submit their methodological or empirical articles (see Chapter 8) have guidelines reviewers use to assess the quality of manuscripts. Also, funding agencies set forth the criteria that their reviewers will use to assess an application or proposal for funding. These criteria are often published in easily accessed websites. For book publishers, we can look to certain websites (e.g., http://mmr.sagepub.com) to find several guidelines for quality in mixed methods today.

Finally, faculty advisers have standards that they use to assess the quality of doctoral dissertations, theses, and research reports. Sometimes these standards reflect their interest in good prose, or they may speak to specific content topics (e.g., is the literature adequately reviewed?). With mixed methods as a new methodology area, and with the availability of a small but growing list of mixed methods courses, faculty may or may not have a firm list of standards they use to evaluate a mixed methods study. They may rely on published standards from journals, from guidelines advanced by federal agencies, or even from journal articles on quality in mixed methods. As more faculty become familiar with the basic tenets of mixed methods (e.g., the core characteristics advanced in Chapter 1), greater consensus may emerge about how to assess the quality of a mixed methods study.

❖ SHOULD WE HAVE STANDARDS?

I am sure that scholars are quite divided on this issue. It will be helpful to review the pros and cons of using standards to assess the quality of mixed methods research. On the positive side, it is true that reviewers of journal articles need some standards to apply when they review a mixed methods project. With a large editorial board and many occasional reviewers that help to assess manuscripts, having some standards is helpful. The same applies to reviewers for federal funding agencies (and private foundations).

With so many reviewers on board to review applications, the agencies have taken the stand that standards are needed so that arbitrary decisions are not made as to whether a mixed methods study is funded or not.

Standards seem to have a different reading from field to field. In the health sciences, the use of standards is pervasive, whether these are protocols for screening, diagnosis, or surgical procedures. Protocols are a way of life for those working in the health sciences. Therefore, having standards in mixed methods makes sense, and is quite within the working life of the health science clinician and researcher. In the social sciences, on the other hand, protocols, checklists, and standards are less likely to be used. The social science researcher may use an instrument developed by another scholar, but likely the instrument will be adapted to "fit" the participants under study.

The contexts for studying people differ widely, and this is certainly clear in the global arena, where the local conditions greatly affect the research process. Qualitative researchers in the social and behavioral sciences have for years believed in an open-ended process of gathering information that allows participants to provide their views rather than restricting them through a predetermined set of questions or instruments. Quantitative researchers are more inclined to use and believe in standards, and they operate on the assumption that patterns of behavior, for example, fit into some ordered sequence that can be measured and assessed, regardless of the specific context of the individuals.

Finally, another argument for standards often comes from beginning researchers who need to have clear guidelines for how to proceed and how their work will be evaluated. They do not have the experience to innovate and create because they are simply not familiar with the ground rules.

The other side, of course, is to look at the disadvantages of having standards or guidelines in research approaches. Guidelines are creations of individuals, groups, funding agencies, faculty committees, and so forth. Who is capable of deciding whether these individuals and groups know what they are doing? It becomes a question of power, and of who controls the generation of knowledge. Sometimes the individuals generating the guidelines are after their own good; they may want to control the nature of research to advance their own agendas. Thus, guidelines can sometimes lead to undesirable outcomes.

Another downside of guidelines is that they create a structure around what is acceptable and what is not. This may limit the creativity of individuals and actually slow down the adoption of mixed methods. The experienced researcher may feel the need to fashion his or her mixed methods project within the guidelines, thus limiting the uniqueness that he or she may bring to mixed methods. Unquestionably, experienced researchers do not like to be bounded by standards and desire freedom in creating their mixed methods projects. These researchers may attempt to master the basics of a methodology and then wish to create projects outside of these structures to advance their studies.

Finally, arguing against standards or guidelines is the idea that there is simply no agreement on what these guidelines should be. The classic case in mixed methods was the article by Johnson, Onwuegbuzie, and Turner (2007), who attempted to forge a single definition of mixed methods by asking 19 different scholars for their working definition. As you read through these definitions, you begin to see that on something so basic as a definition of mixed methods, scholars differ, and that a consensus is difficult to develop.

My particular stance lies more in the direction of having standards of quality for mixed methods. I feel that:

- Standards will advance the field of mixed methods by providing reviewers and evaluators with a set of guidelines that can be helpful in assessing quality.
- Standards are imperative in the health sciences, where guidelines and protocols are central to clinical and medical practice and research.
- Standards need to be generally stated to allow the broadest application possible across the social, behavioral, and health sciences.

Consequently, you will find in my books checklists and discussions about the array of evaluation standards being used. I have included these because of my work in the health sciences and because they are helpful to beginning researchers (or so I have been told).

❖ CRITERIA I USED AS COEDITOR OF *JMMR*

When my colleagues and I founded the *Journal of Mixed Methods Research*, we of course needed guidelines for reviewers of manuscripts. Our reviewer pool consisted of the approximately 25 reviewers on the editorial board plus some 200 occasional reviewers on special topics and content areas, from different places around the world. Our journal was both interdisciplinary and international in scope. Further, as we developed the journal, we saw two types of manuscripts coming in: empirical articles in which the authors studied a specific topic and used mixed methods as the methodology for studying the topic; and methodological articles, in which the authors conveyed information advancing the practice of mixed methods (e.g., a methodological paper on validity or on types of designs) (see Chapter 8).

When you look at the guidelines for authors submitting manuscripts and for reviewers of those manuscripts, you can see standards being used in two ways: as a definition of the types of articles that constitute an empirical article and those that constitute a methodological article, and the review criteria for both types of articles. You can go to the SAGE Publications website for the *Journal of Mixed Methods Research* and see these guidelines (www.sagepub.com/journals/Journal201775#tabview=manuscriptSubmiss ion). It might be helpful to review them to assess their level of specificity.

JMMR Criteria for Empirical Articles

The general definition of an empirical mixed methods article is one that reports empirical mixed methods research in the social, behavioral, health, or human sciences. These manuscripts must:

- fit the definition of mixed methods research by reporting the collection and analysis of data, integrating the findings, and drawing inferences using both qualitative and quantitative approaches or methods;
- explicitly integrate the quantitative and qualitative aspects of the study; and
- discuss how they add to the literature on mixed methods research in addition to making a contribution to a substantive area in the scholar's field of inquiry.

Original research manuscripts that do not show integration or discuss how they add to the mixed methods literature are to be returned to the author(s).
The review criteria include:

- Noteworthiness of the problem
- Theoretical framework
- Fit of questions to mixed methods design
- Mixed methods design
- Mixed methods sampling
- Mixed methods analysis and integration
- Insightfulness of discussion
- Writing quality

- Quality of conclusions
- Contribution to mixed methods literature
- Interest to *JMMR* readership

JMMR Criteria for Methodological/Theoretical Articles

These articles are defined as discussing methodological or theoretical issues that advance knowledge about mixed methods research. They must:

- address an important mixed methods topic;
- adequately incorporate existing literature; and
- contribute to our understanding of mixed methods research.

The review criteria include:

- Whether it addresses an important topic
- Adequacy of the literature
- Soundness of the argument
- Originality of the suggestions
- Writing quality
- Contribution to mixed methods literature
- Interest to *JMMR* readership

These guidelines seem to set forth standards for researchers but advance ideas in the most general terms. For example, the type of design is not specified in the empirical article guidelines, nor is the topic constrained in the methodological article. The definitions of both types of articles create some helpful boundaries in terms of the manuscript forms sought by the journal.

❖ STANDARDS AVAILABLE FOR MIXED METHODS RESEARCH

Research standards are not new to journals, funding agencies, private foundations, disciplines or fields, or workshops. What is new, however, is their entrance into mixed methods. For example, the National Science Foundation issued *The 2002 User-Friendly Handbook for Project Evaluation* (www.nsf.gov/pubs/2002/nsf02057/start.htm), which contained a section on mixed methods evaluations. In 2008, the Robert Wood Johnson website for the Qualitative Research Guidelines Project (www.qualres.org/) provided a practical set of guidelines for the qualitative component of mixed methods projects. These guidelines not only were used as a model for designing website research methods content but also provided the NIH Office of Behavioral and Social Science helpful suggestions in identifying "best practices" for qualitative methods (as mentioned in Chapter 6; see discussion below). In 2010, USAID issued tips for conducting mixed methods evaluations, and articles have been written about basic guidelines for mixed methods research in medical education (Schifferdecker & Reed, 2009). Workshops, in a way, advance how mixed methods is being and perhaps should be conducted; an example is the 2012 National Institutes of Health (NIH) workshop on "Using Mixed Methods to Optimize Dissemination and Implementation of Health Interventions."

In short, we have an emerging set of guidelines for mixed methods research, and individuals writing the literature on mixed methods have added their voices to this trend. Consistent with what might be expected in regard to guidelines, mixed methods writers have advanced several lists of expectations.

As shown in Table 9.1, I present three standards from the literature. A quick review of these three guidelines indicates that they are not far from the *JMMR* criteria set forth earlier. Creswell and Plano Clark's (2011) set does seem to reflect the journal's definition of mixed methods research and its core characteristics. The O'Cathain, Murphy, and Nicholl (2008b) list is more general, and it relates closely to what might be expected in any research study. The Schifferdecker and Reed (2009) recommendations probably fall somewhere in the middle between the first two: They speak to mixed methods and specific aspects, such as study design and sampling, but do not bind authors to detailed procedures. Of additional interest in Table 9.1 are recommendations to advance a justification for mixed methods, to set realistic goals for the study, to use software for analysis, and to establish limitations and insights from the study.

NIH RECOMMENDATIONS ❖ FOR "BEST PRACTICES"

These three sets of recommendations were included in the recent recommendations for "Best Practices for Mixed Methods Research in the Health Sciences," as introduced earlier in Chapter 6. These recommendations

Table 9.1 A Comparison of Different Criteria
for Evaluating a Mixed Methods Study

Criteria	Creswell & Plano Clark (2011)	O'Cathain, Murphy, & Nicholl (2008b)	Schifferdecker & Reed (2009)
Mixed methods design	Use a mixed methods design	Describe the design in terms of purpose, priority, sequence	Identify the study design
The methods	Employ rigorous quantitative and qualitative methods	Describe methods in terms of sampling, data collection, data analysis	Decide on prominence of each data type, analysis, and results
Data collection and analysis	Collect both quantitative and qualitative data and analyze them		Develop sampling strategies and determine how and when data are collected, analyzed, integrated
Integrate data	Merge, embed, or connect the databases	Describe where and how integration occurs	
Others	Use consistent mixed methods terms	Describe justification for mixed methods; describe limitations and insights from study	Set realistic time requirements; use software; review mixed methods articles to generate ideas

flowed from an NIH Office of Behavioral and Social Science Research (OBSSR) working group of 18 individuals representing NIH institutes, program officers, and mixed methods specialists in the social, behavioral, and health sciences. This working group was chaired by me, Ann Klassen of Drexel University, Vicki Plano Clark of the University of Cincinnati, and Kate Smith of Johns Hopkins University. Early in the design of these recommendations, it was felt that the "practices" should address the basic features of mixed methods; advance recommendations for writing a mixed methods application for the various NIH granting mechanisms (R grant,

K grant, Center grant, and so forth); and establish criteria that evaluators might use when reviewing an application for funding for mixed methods research. It was also acknowledged early in the deliberations that the 2001 NIH OBSSR report, *Qualitative Methods in Health Research: Opportunities and Considerations in Application and Review*, which contained a short section on mixed methods studies, was not sufficient to reflect the current state of the art in mixed methods research.

The final report provides recommendations for conducting mixed methods research in the health sciences. The topics of the report reflect this triple orientation toward informing the reader about the nature of this form of inquiry, giving suggestions for writing applications, and providing a checklist for reviewers to use. It is informative to review the topics that unfolded in this report by looking at the table of contents:

Best Practices for Mixed Methods Research in the Health Sciences

http://obssr.od.nih.gov/mixed_methods_research/

TABLE OF CONTENTS

- Acknowledgement
- Introduction and Background
- The Need for Best Practices
- The Nature and Design of Mixed Methods Research
- Teamwork, Infrastructure, Resources, and Training for Mixed Methods Research
- Developing an R Series Plan That Incorporates Mixed Methods Research
- Beyond the R Series – High-Quality Mixed Methods Activities in Successful Fellowship, Career, Training, and Center Grant Applications
- Reviewing Mixed Methods Applications
- Overall Recommendations
- Appendix A. NIH Working Group on Developing Best Practices for Mixed Methods Research

I highlight here the checklist in the section on "Reviewing Mixed Methods Applications." This checklist related to the major components being evaluated by NIH reviewers of applications: the significance of the study, the investigator(s), the innovation, the approach, and the environment. In addition, the items on this checklist were adapted to fit the latest thinking about mixed methods research. For example, under "Significance," one criterion is, "Can the problem be best studied through the multiple perspectives of mixed methods?" Another criterion, under "Approach," is "Is the integration of the methods well described, including the timing, techniques, and responsibilities for integration?" The idea of this checklist is to provide reviewers with guidelines—standards, if you will—that will help them evaluate the quality of applications for NIH funding across the different institutes and centers.

❖ RECOMMENDATIONS FROM THIS CHAPTER

This chapter acknowledged that evaluation standards are being used by journals, books, faculty advisors, and funding agencies. Unquestionably, these standards have both advantages and disadvantages for use, and researchers need to weigh these factors when they seek to evaluate a mixed methods study. Journals seem to have the most specific standards, and I advance those that are being used by the *Journal of Mixed Methods Research*. Of course, these are not the only standards for mixed methods research; others are being promulgated through websites, discipline-based publications, and federal funding agencies and private foundations, as well as through specialized workshops. Moreover, several mixed methods writers have advanced their own standards, ranging from more general guidelines to specific ones. Most recently, NIH through OBSSR convened a working group to develop "best practices" for mixed methods in the health sciences. The general format for these recommendations was to first advance the nature of mixed methods research and then to suggest practices helpful to scholars preparing NIH applications and to reviewers on panels convened by NIH to evaluate the applications. Of special note is the checklist that reviewers might use to evaluate an application. This checklist and the larger report are available on the OBSSR website for public use.

ADDITIONAL READINGS   ❖

Creswell, J. W., Klassen, A. C., Plano Clark, V. L., & Smith, K. C., for the Office of Behavioral and Social Sciences Research. (2011, August). *Best practices for mixed methods research in the health sciences.* Washington, DC: National Institutes of Health. Retrieved from http://obssr.od.nih.gov/mixed_methods_research

Johnson, R. B., Onwuegbuzie, A. J., & Turner, L. A. (2007). Toward a definition of mixed methods research. *Journal of Mixed Methods Research, 1,* 112–133. doi: 10.1177/1558689806298224

O'Cathain, A., Murphy, E., & Nicholl, J. (2008). The quality of mixed methods studies in health services research. *Journal of Health Services Research and Policy, 13*(2), 92–98. doi: 10.1258/jhsrp.2007.007074

CHAPTER 10

THE DEVELOPMENT AND ADVANCEMENT OF MIXED METHODS

❖ TOPICS IN THE CHAPTER

- Scientific developments in mixed methods as a summary of major topics discussed in this book
- The development of mixed methods in this digital age

❖ SCIENTIFIC DEVELOPMENTS

There are several scientific developments in mixed methods research that should be part of the everyday learning of the mixed methods student today. Of course, we now have journals specifically devoted to mixed methods research, such as the *Journal of Mixed Methods Research* and the *International Journal of Multiple Research Approaches*. As a field, mixed methods research has expanded considerably through methodological writings in different fields and in leading journals. It is quite popular in the health sciences now, and it has been present throughout the social sciences. It has also expanded internationally with interests in many regions of the world, such as Africa (e.g., South Africa) and Southeast Asia (e.g., Thailand). It is often seen as having Anglo-American roots, especially given the origin of the Mixed Methods International Conference in England and the many European and American books out now that discuss the mixed methods field.

What sets mixed methods today apart from mixed methods, say, five years ago, are the many empirical mixed methods studies being published in academic journals. We now have many exemplar studies to draw on to learn how mixed methods works. Supporting this is the interest by private foundations (through workshops) and the federal government (through websites of "best practices" advancing how to conduct rigorous mixed methods investigations). We would add to this the new courses on mixed methods research emerging on many large, distinguished campuses across the United States and England. In the spring of 2014, Harvard offered a mixed methods course in its Department of Global Health and Social Medicine.

What, then, are some of the scientific developments that have emerged to enhance the credibility and use of mixed methods?

Core Characteristics

We now have a good sense of what constitutes the core characteristics of mixed methods research. Although writers may take a more philosophical or theoretical view of this field, my approach has always been to work outward from the methods. So, in this spirit, mixed methods involves, as discussed in Chapter 1: (a) collecting and analyzing quantitative and qualitative data in response to open- and closed-ended research questions or hypotheses, (b) using rigorous methods for both quantitative and qualitative procedures, (c) integrating the two databases and interpreting the results using specific types of mixed methods designs, and (d) incorporating—at times—various theoretical perspectives and making explicit the philosophical foundation of the research. On the reverse side, we also know what mixed methods is not—and the most apparent problem today is that researchers collect both quantitative and qualitative data, do not integrate the two databases, and call it mixed methods. Mixed methods actually involves the integration of the two databases, which is a key element of conducting this form of research.

Terminology

Another scientific development in the mixed methods field has been the adoption of specific terminology. In all methodologies, the researchers have developed their own language, and mixed methods is no exception. In fact, at the back of most mixed methods books, you will see a glossary of terms, and these terms often are similar from one text to another (see the Glossary at the end of this book). A key term is *mixed methods* itself. This kind of research has been called other names—such as *multimethod, integrated,* or *mixed* research—but today, with the establishment of the *Handbook* (Tashakkori & Teddlie, 2010), the *Journal of Mixed Methods Research* (JMMR), and the Mixed Method International Research Association, we seem to have designated the term *mixed methods* as a standard label.

The Value of Mixed Methods

Increasingly today, attention is focusing more on the "value" of mixed methods. Researchers ask: "What is the value of mixed methods over using only quantitative research or only qualitative research?" We would have to acknowledge that mixed methods researchers have not always been explicit about this value when writing methodological or empirical articles. A scan of empirical mixed methods studies, however, would reveal that some authors mention the value of mixed methods research. Take, for example, the article by Farquhar, Ewing, and Booth (2011). They include a table that specifies how mixed methods added to their study, such as by teasing out important elements of their intervention, extending beyond the limitations of quantitative research, and using qualitative data to compare with their quantitative results. We think about the value questions in terms of general "value," such as contribution of a better understanding of the problem than what might be provided by quantitative or qualitative research alone. At a more specific level, the benefit might be that qualitative data help to explain the quantitative results, or that starting a project qualitatively is the best way to explore the types of questions that need to be asked, will help to shape a program or a set of intervention activities that might actually work, or will yield new variables that may not have occurred to researchers before the study began or were not apparent in the literature. Chapter 2 introduced the reasons or rationale for using mixed methods as an important step in designing a mixed methods study.

Advances in Research Designs

No topic has been more extensively discussed in the literature of mixed methods than research designs. Many types of designs have been introduced over the years, and they come with different labels, different procedures, and different levels of complexity. We tend to think in terms of three basic designs: convergent, explanatory sequential, and exploratory sequential designs. Convergent designs involve merging the two databases; explanatory sequential designs involve following quantitative results with qualitative data to explain the results in more detail; and exploratory sequential designs involve starting qualitatively and building toward a quantitative phase, such as in the design of a quantitative instrument. Advanced designs include these basic designs but add something more. For example, added to a basic design might be an experimental intervention framework, an advocacy or social justice perspective, or a program evaluation dimension. What is also interesting about the designs today is that we have good diagrams of the procedures that researchers might use in their presentations or in their papers. And procedures have now been developed for conducting these designs (i.e., the steps involved have been delineated), and potential threats to validity in conducting the designs have been identified. In Chapter 4, I introduced these designs and provided a definition, description of procedures, and diagram for each of them.

Skills Required for Conducting Mixed Methods Research

We know that mixed methods research takes time and resources; multiple forms of data are collected and multiple procedures of data analysis are conducted. Thus, challenges are inherent in carrying out this form of inquiry. Other challenges we are aware of today include deficient skills and diverging philosophical orientations in investigators. For individuals skilled in quantitative approaches, such as epidemiologists and biostatisticians, we need to provide basic skills in qualitative research. Qualitative researchers need to become comfortable with statistics and the value of using numbers in investigations to map trends, relate variables, or compare groups. In Chapter 3, I reviewed the skills required to conduct mixed methods research.

Use of Philosophy and Theory

Much discussion has occurred among the mixed methods community about the value, use, and types of philosophical orientations and the use of theory. Many philosophical orientations have been advanced as providing the core foundation for mixed methods research. Some writers argue for a single philosophy, while others discuss multiple philosophies. New philosophies are developing all the time, and a key question for mixed methods investigators is whether they make their philosophical assumptions explicit in their studies. This approach, of course, differs from field to field. In terms of theory, many social and behavioral theories have been used as a framework for mixed methods research. One—community-based participatory research (CBPR)—is popular in community studies, and it provides a framework for involving community members in all aspects of the study. In addition to social and behavioral theories, we see many transformation or advocacy types of theories, such as feminist theory, disability theory, and racial theory. These also provide a framework surrounding a mixed methods approach. There has been recent discussion about how to weave these frameworks—social, behavioral, or transformative—into a mixed methods study and how to write up such a study. In Chapter 2, I asked you to consider adding steps to your mixed methods design in order to specify a worldview and/or a theory.

Mixed Methods Research Questions

Another innovation in mixed methods is a new type of research question that is not found in any research methods book to date: a mixed methods question. If we are using a specific mixed methods design, then we are asking a question that is neither quantitative nor qualitative, but a combination of these two approaches. In a good mixed methods study, we need to specify this question as well as the quantitative and qualitative questions, and to link this mixed methods question into the type of design being used in the study. In Chapter 6, I introduced the idea of a mixed methods question and how to link it to the type of mixed methods design being used in a study.

Joint Displays

More and more attention today is being given to how to analyze the qualitative and quantitative data in tandem. How do we merge or integrate, for example, text data from qualitative research with numeric data from quantitative data? To do this, we turn to joint displays. The two forms of data might be jointly displayed in a discussion (called side-by-side joint display), in a graph, or in a table. We have made major inroads in using joint displays, where we might, for example, array the themes on one dimension and the categories of quantitative data on another dimension. Computer software has pushed us forward in creating these joint displays. One qualitative software product, MAXQDA (Verbi GmbH, 2013), now has a pull-down menu for mixed methods to facilitate the analysis of mixed methods data and the creation of these displays. In Chapter 7, I introduced these joint displays, provided an example of one, and talked about their importance in a mixed methods study.

Writing and Publishing Mixed Methods Studies

Since many published empirical mixed methods studies are available in the literature, we have good models for how to write mixed methods journal articles and what mixed methods components to include in them. For example, we now pay attention to the creation of a good mixed methods title, purpose statement, and research questions (quantitative, qualitative, and mixed methods). Also, we include detailed discussion about mixed methods procedures, such as the types of quantitative and qualitative data and how they are integrated, and use mixed methods references. There have been some recommendations for how to publish mixed methods studies, especially when the journal reviewers call for short articles of, say, 3,000 words. We are also learning about how to publish these mixed methods studies in separate publications, such as by writing a quantitative article, a qualitative article, and an overview mixed methods article. We might add to these articles a methodological article that addresses the unique research methods features of our study. We also know today how to abbreviate the overview mixed methods article so that it can be condensed into a short study somewhere between 3,000 and 6,000 words. Such condensation is not needed in some publications, such as social science mixed methods journals. For example, for the *Journal of Mixed Methods Research*, we allowed researchers the space of 8,000 to 10,000 words for their articles. In Chapter 8, I reviewed how to write a mixed methods article for publication and specifically addressed how to write the methods, results, and discussion sections for studies built on each of the major mixed methods designs.

Standards of Quality

Finally, standards for evaluating the quality of a mixed methods study are now being produced. These should not be seen as rigid templates, but as general guidelines for use. In the mixed methods field, several authors have created useful guidelines, and more recently, the federal government has issued some quality practices. The National Science Foundation has a document providing guidelines for mixed methods research, and the National Institutes of Health (Office of Behavioral and Social Science Research) has provided recommendations on a website for mixed methods "best practices" in the health sciences. How rigidly we need to specify how mixed methods works is, of course, open to debate, but we find that often graduate students appreciate having quality guidelines as they develop proposals for theses and dissertations, conference presentations, journal article submissions, and applications for private and public funds. Chapter 9 discussed standards of quality for mixed methods projects and made specific recommendations about components of mixed methods to use in high-quality studies.

❖ MIXED METHODS IN THE DIGITAL AGE

In any workshop, course, or book that is written about mixed methods today, the content needs to address the important scientific procedures that have evolved during the last 10 or so years. These procedures build on important ways of conveying research methods, such as by outlining multiple approaches, comparing the different approaches side by side, using practical examples, and above all else, writing in a user-friendly way. Moreover, research methods today need to fully utilize the technologies available. Indeed, mixed methods might be seen as the first major research methodology to fully utilize digital capabilities such as digital flowcharts, computer software analysis, and web communication for individuals around the world who may not have access to current books, conference workshops, and content specialists. These innovations indicate the advancement of a methodology in a way that was not available to other methodologies emerging during the 1970s, 1980s, or 1990s (e.g., meta-analysis, participatory action research). This means that the word about mixed methods will spread rapidly across disciplines and around the world. Those seeking to use mixed methods need to keep abreast of the latest scientific developments in order to plan and conduct a good mixed methods project.

RECOMMENDATIONS FROM THIS CHAPTER   ❖

It is important to plan a mixed methods project that takes advantage of some of the technological advancements that have come about over the last few years. Here are some questions you might ask yourself:

- Am I advancing a study that contains the core characteristics of mixed methods research?
- Am I familiar with and using research terms frequently used in the mixed methods field?
- Am I familiar with the arguments for convincing others of the value of mixed methods research?
- Am I using a recognized mixed methods design?
- Do I have an understanding of some of the challenges inherent in using the design?
- Will I incorporate philosophy into my study? Will I have a theory?
- What mixed methods research question will I answer with my mixed methods design?
- How will I display the integration of the quantitative and qualitative data?
- Am I familiar with the mixed methods components that go into a published study?
- How will I determine whether I have a high-quality study?

ADDITIONAL READINGS   ❖

To learn about innovations in mixed methods, see:

Creswell, J. W. (in press). Revisiting mixed methods and advancing scientific practices. In S. N. Hesse-Biber and R. B. Johnson (Eds.), *The Oxford handbook of mixed and multiple research methods*. Oxford, UK: Oxford University Press.

For help in publishing a mixed methods journal article, consult:

Stange, K. C., Crabtree, B. F., & Miller, W. L. (2006). Publishing multimethod research. *Annals of Family Medicine, 4*, 292–294.

To understand the "best practice" recommendations of the National Institutes of Health's Office of Behavioral and Social Science Research, go to:

Creswell, J. W., Klassen, A. C., Plano Clark, V. L., & Smith, K. C., for the Office of Behavioral and Social Sciences Research. (2011, August). *Best practices for mixed methods research in the health sciences.* Washington, DC: National Institutes of Health. Retrieved from: http://obssr.od.nih.gov/mixed_methods_research

A major handbook on mixed methods research is:

Tashakkori, A., & Teddlie, C. (Eds.) (2010). *SAGE handbook of mixed methods in social and behavioral research.* (2nd ed.). Thousand Oaks, CA: Sage.

Major journals devoted to mixed methods research are:

Journal of Mixed Methods Research (http://mmr.sagepub.com/)
International Journal of Multiple Research Approaches (http://pubs.e-contentman agement.com/loi/mra)

For examples of joint displays, see:

Creswell, J. W., & Plano Clark, V. L. (2011). *Designing and conducting mixed methods research* (2nd ed.). Thousand Oaks, CA: Sage.
Plano Clark, V. L., Garrett, A. L., & Leslie-Pelecky, D. L. (2009). Applying three strategies for integrating quantitative and qualitative databases in a mixed methods study of a nontraditional graduate education program. *Field Methods, 22,* 154–174.

REFERENCES

Brannen, J., & Moss, G. (2012). Critical issues in designing mixed methods policy research. *American Behavioral Scientist, 56*, 789-801. doi: 10.1177/0002764211433796

Brown, J., Sorrell, J. H., McClaren, J., & Creswell, J. W. (2006). Waiting for a liver transplant. *Qualitative Health Research, 16*, 119-136. doi: 10.1177/1049732305284011

Bryman, A. (2006). Integrating quantitative and qualitative research: How is it done? *Qualitative Research, 6*, 97-113. doi: 10.1177/1468794106058877

Creswell, J. W. (2012). *Educational research: Planning, conducting, and evaluating quantitative and qualitative research* (4th ed.). Boston, MA: Pearson.

Creswell, J. W. (2013). *Qualitative inquiry and research design: Choosing among five approaches* (3rd ed.). Thousand Oaks, CA: Sage.

Creswell, J. W. (2014). *Research design: Qualitative, quantitative, and mixed methods approaches* (4th ed.). Thousand Oaks, CA: Sage.

Creswell, J. W. (in press). Revisiting mixed methods and advancing scientific practices. In S. N. Hesse-Biber & R. B. Johnson (Eds.), *The Oxford handbook of mixed and multiple research methods*. Oxford, UK: Oxford University Press.

Creswell, J. W., Fetters, M. D., Plano Clark, V. L., & Morales, A. (2009). Mixed methods intervention trials. In S. Andrew & E. J. Halcomb (Eds.), *Mixed methods research for nursing and the health sciences* (pp. 161-180). Oxford, UK: John Wiley & Sons.

Creswell, J. W., Klassen, A. C., Plano Clark, V. L., & Smith, K. C. (2011). Best practices for mixed methods research in the health sciences. Washington, DC: National Institutes of Health. Available online: http://obssr.od.nih.gov/mixed_methods_research/

Creswell, J. W., & Plano Clark, V. L. (2011). *Designing and conducting mixed methods research* (2nd ed.). Thousand Oaks, CA: Sage.

Creswell, J. W., & Zhang, W. (2009). The application of mixed methods designs to trauma research. *Journal of Traumatic Stress, 22*, 612-621. doi: 10.1002/jts.20479

Dahlberg, B., Wittink, M. N., & Gallo, J. J. (2010). Funding and publishing integrated studies: Writing effective mixed methods manuscripts and grant proposals. In A. Tashakkori & C. Teddlie (Eds.), *SAGE handbook of mixed methods in social and behavioral research*. Thousand Oaks, CA: Sage.

DeVellis, R. F. (2012). *Scale development: Theory and applications* (3rd ed.). Thousand Oaks, CA: Sage.

Farquhar, M. C., Ewing, G., & Booth, S. (2011). Using mixed methods to develop and evaluate complex interventions in palliative care research. *Palliative Medicine, 25*, 748-757. doi: 10.1177/0269216311417919

Fetters, M. D., Curry, L. A., & Creswell, J. W. (2013). Achieving integration in mixed methods designs—Principles and practices. *Health Services Research, 48*, 2134-2156. doi: 10.1111/1475-6773.12117

Fowler, F. J., Jr. (2008). *Survey research methods* (4th ed.). Thousand Oaks, CA: Sage.

Frechtling, J. (2002). The 2002 user-friendly handbook for project evaluation Arlington, VA: The National Science Foundation. Available online: http://www.nsf.gov/pubs/2002/nsf02057/start.htm

Guba, E. G. (1990). The alternative paradigm dialog. In E. G. Guba (Ed.), *The paradigm dialog* (pp. 17-30). Newbury Park, CA: Sage.

Guetterman, T., Creswell, J. W., & Kuckartz, U. (in press). Using visual displays in mixed methods research. In M. McCrudden, G. Schraw, and C. Buckendahl (Eds.), *Use of visual displays in research and testing: Coding, interpreting, and reporting data*. Charlotte, NC: Information Age Publishing.

Ivankova, N. V., Creswell, J. W., & Stick, S. L. (2006). Using mixed-methods sequential explanatory design: From theory to practice. *Field Methods, 18*, 3-20. doi: 10.1177/1525822X05282260

Ivankova, N. V., & Stick, S. L. (2007). Students' persistence in a distributed doctoral program in educational leadership in higher education: A mixed methods study. *Research in Higher Education, 48*, 93-135. doi: 10.1007/s11162-006-9025-4

Johnson, R. B., Onwuegbuzie, A. J., & Turner, L. A. (2007). Toward a definition of mixed methods research. *Journal of Mixed Methods Research, 1*, 112-133. doi: 10.1177/1558689806298224

Kuhn, T. S. (1962). *The structure of scientific revolutions*. Chicago, IL: University of Chicago Press.

Leech, N. L., Dellinger, A. B., Brannagan, K. B., & Tanaka, H. (2009). Evaluating mixed research studies: A mixed methods approach. *Journal of Mixed Methods Research, 4*, 17-31. doi: 10.1177/1558689809345262

Lipsey, M. W. (1990). *Design sensitivity: Statistical power for experimental research*. Newbury Park, CA: Sage.

Maxwell, J. A. (2013). *Qualitative research design: An interactive approach* (3rd ed.). Thousand Oaks, CA: Sage.

Morse, J. M. (1991). Approaches to qualitative-quantitative methodological triangulation. *Nursing Research, 40*, 120-123.

Morse, J. M. (2003). Principles of mixed methods and multimethod research design. In A. Tashakkori & C. Teddlie (Eds.), *Handbook of mixed methods in social & behavioral research* (pp. 189-208). Thousand Oaks, CA: Sage.

Morse, J. M., & Niehaus, L. (2009). *Mixed methods design: Principles and procedures*. Walnut Creek, CA: Left Coast Press.

O'Cathain, A. (2009). Reporting mixed methods projects. In S. Andrew & E. J. Halcomb (Eds.), *Mixed methods research for nursing and the health sciences* (pp. 135-158). West Sussex, UK: Blackwell.

O'Cathain, A., Murphy, E., & Nicholl, J. (2008a). Multidisciplinary, interdisciplinary, or dysfunctional? Team working in mixed-methods research. *Qualitative Health Research, 18*, 1574-1585.

O'Cathain, A., Murphy, E., & Nicholl, J. (2008b). The quality of mixed methods studies in health services research. *Journal of Health Services Research & Policy, 13*, 92-98. doi: 10.1258/jhsrp.2007.007074

Onwuegbuzie, A. J. (2012) Putting the MIXED back into quantitative and qualitative research in educational research and beyond: Moving towards the "radical middle". *International Journal of Multiple Research Approaches, 6*, 192-219.

Plano Clark, V. L., & Badiee, M. (2010). Research questions in mixed methods research. In A. Tashakkori & C. Teddlie (Eds.), *SAGE Handbook of mixed methods in social & behavioral research* (2nd ed., pp. 275-304). Thousand Oaks, CA: Sage.

Plano Clark, V. L., Garrett, A. L., & Leslie-Pelecky, D. L. (2009). Applying three strategies for integrating quantitative and qualitative databases in a mixed methods study of a nontraditional graduate education program. *Field Methods, 22*, 154-174. doi: 10.1177/1525822X09357174

Rossi, P. H., Lipsey, M. W., & Freeman, H. E. (2004). *Evaluation: A systematic approach*. Thousand Oaks, CA: Sage.

Rossman, G. B., & Wilson, B. L. (1985). Numbers and words: Combining quantitative and qualitative methods in a single large-scale evaluation study. *Evaluation Review, 9*, 627-643. doi: 10.1177/0193841X8500900505

Sandelowski, M. (2003). Tables or tableaux? The challenges of writing and reading mixed methods studies. In A. Tashakkori & C. Teddlie (Eds.), *Handbook of mixed methods in social & behavioral research* (pp. 321-350). Thousand Oaks, CA: Sage.

Schifferdecker, K. E., & Reed, V. A. (2009). Using mixed methods research in medical education: Basic guidelines for researchers. *Medical Education, 43*, 637-644. doi: 10.1111/j.1365-2923.2009.03386.x

Schulz, K. F., Altman, D. G., & Moher, D. (2010). CONSORT 2010 Statement: Updated Guidelines for Reporting Parallel Group Randomized Trials. *Annals of Internal Medicine, 152*, 726-732. doi: 10.7326/0003-4819-152-11-201006010-00232

Shadish, W. R., Cook, T. D., & Campbell, D. T. (2002). *Experimental and quasi-experimental designs for generalized causal inference*. Boston: Houghton Mifflin.

Stange, K. C., Crabtree, B. F., & Miller, W. L. (2006). Publishing multimethod research. *Annals of Family Medicine, 4*, 292-294. doi: 10.1370/afm.615

Stewart, M., Makwarimba, E., Barnfather, A., Letourneau, N., & Neufeld, A. (2008). Researching reducing health disparities: Mixed-methods approaches. *Social Science & Medicine, 66*, 1406-1417. doi: 10.1016/j.socscimed.2007.11.021

Tashakkori, A., & Teddlie, C. (Eds.). (2010). *SAGE handbook of mixed methods in social & behavioral research* (2nd ed.). Thousand Oaks, CA: Sage.

Verbi GmbH. (2013). MAXQDA. Retrieved from http://www.maxqda.com/

Wittink, M. N., Barg, F. K., & Gallo, J. J. (2006). Unwritten rules of talking to doctors about depression: Integrating qualitative and quantitative methods. *Annals of Family Medicine, 4*, 302-309. doi: 10.1370/afm.558

GLOSSARY

Advanced designs – These designs utilize advanced features to add to the basic designs in mixed methods research (convergent, explanatory, or exploratory). What might be added to these designs would be to build them into a larger framework (e.g., a convergent procedure is built into an experimental design, or to add a convergent procedure into a theory, such as feminist theory), or to build them into an overall program of inquiry that spans a period of time (multiple studies are used in a longitudinal program of research).

Basic designs – These are designs used in all mixed methods studies. They consist of the convergent design with the intent to merge quantitative and qualitative data; the explanatory sequential design in which the intent is to explain quantitative results with qualitative data; and the exploratory design in which the intent is to first explore and then build in a quantitative phase to test the qualitative themes with a larger *N*.

Convergent design – This is one of the three basic designs in mixed methods research. It involves the separate collection of both quantitative and qualitative data, distinct analyses, and the merging of the two databases to compare their results. Typically, researchers attempt to explain or resolve any differences between the two databases.

Data transformation – Data transformation is when the mixed methods researcher collects qualitative data (e.g., interview data) and then transforms it into quantitative data (e.g., counts of the number of times a code appears in the database). In mixed methods research, the transformed qualitative data (the new quantitative database) is then compared or combined with another quantitative database.

Diagram of procedures – In mixed methods research, investigators often draw diagrams of their mixed methods designs. These diagrams indicate the flow of activities, the specific steps taken in the procedures of data collection, data analysis, and interpretation, and sometimes they include the notation of QUAL and QUAN (or other notation) used in the field of mixed methods research.

Epistemology – This concept is related to the type of evidence used to make claims, including the relationship between the researcher and participants (e.g., impartial and distant or collaborative).

Explanatory sequential design – This basic design has the intent of first using quantitative methods and then using qualitative methods to help *explain* the quantitative results in more depth. This is a popular, straightforward design in mixed methods.

Exploratory sequential design – This is one of the three basic designs in mixed methods research. It typically involves three phases: in the first phase the researcher starts with qualitative data collection to explore a topic. The qualitative data are then analyzed, and the results are used in phase two to build a quantitative data collection procedure. This procedure may be the design of a quantitative instrument, an intervention procedure, or the development of quantitative variables. This second phase is then followed by a third phase in which the quantitative instrument, intervention, or variables are used in a quantitative data collection and analysis procedure.

Integration – In mixed methods research, integration refers to how one brings together the qualitative and quantitative results in a mixed methods study. The way the researcher combines the data needs to relate to the type of mixed methods design used. Types of integration include merging, explaining, building, and embedding.

Intervention design – This advanced design builds on one of the basic designs. The intent of this design is to study a problem by conducting an experiment or an intervention trial and adding qualitative data into it. The researcher collects qualitative data before, during, or after an experiment and integrates it through embedding.

Joint display – This is the procedure, typically used in a convergent design, to merge the quantitative and qualitative data. A joint display is a table or a graph that portrays results from both the quantitative and qualitative data collection (e.g., qualitative themes are arrayed against a quantitative categorical variable, or, given constructs examined in a study, both qualitative interviews and quantitative survey items are arrayed in columns to reflect results about the constructs).

Methodology – The process of research stretching from philosophy through interpretation and dissemination.

Methods – The specific procedures of data collection, analysis, and interpretation.

Mixed methods design – A design encompasses all aspects of the procedures for a mixed methods study from the philosophy, to the questions, and on to the data collection, analysis, and interpretation. Within the design, the methods in mixed methods research are the procedures that the researcher uses to collect data, analyze the data, represent the data (e.g., tables, figures), and interpret the data.

Mixed methods research – An approach to research in the social, behavioral, and health sciences in which the investigator gathers both quantitative (closed-ended) and qualitative (open-ended) data, integrates the two, and then draws interpretations based on the combined strengths of both sets of data to understand research problems.

Mixed methods research question – In mixed methods research this is the question being answered by the mixed methods design. The mixed methods question might be: "how do the two databases compare?" (convergent design), "how are the quantitative results explained by the qualitative findings" (explanatory sequential design), "how can the exploratory themes (collected on a small group) be generalized to a large sample of a population" (exploratory sequential design).

Mixed methods sampling – The procedures for sampling within a particular design. These include good quantitative sampling, qualitative sampling, and mixed methods sampling that relate to a specific type of basic or advanced design.

Multistage evaluation design – This design is an advanced design, building on one or more of the basic designs. The intent of this design is to conduct a study over time that evaluates the success of a program or activities implemented into a setting. The design involves a longitudinal study of many stages conducted over time with a central objective of the sustained line of inquiry.

Ontology – This concept is the nature of reality (e.g., multiple or singular realities) in a research study.

Pragmatism – Pragmatism is a philosophy of research focused on consequences of research, the problem, and what works in real-world practice.

Qualitative data – This is the type of data collected in a qualitative study. It is often referred to as "text" data, such as the type of information collected and then transcribed in interviews. It could also be "image" data, such as in the use of photographs or videos. At a broader level, we can consider qualitative data as "open-ended" data, in that the researcher gathers information from participants without specifying their response categories (such as strongly agree to strongly disagree). The typical forms of qualitative data are: open-ended interview data; open-ended observation data; documents, such as diaries, letters, or minutes of meetings; and audio-visual materials, such as photographs, videotapes, artifacts, and website information.

Quantitative data – This is the type of data collected in a quantitative study. It is often referred to as "numeric" data or "numbers." At a broader level, it should be seen as "closed-ended" information, such as the type of information obtained on a survey when participants check the correct response. Numeric data can be information reported on instruments, information checked by the researchers as they observe using a checklist, or numbered information available on reports or documents (e.g., census data, attendance data).

Random sampling – An approach to sampling in quantitative research in which the researcher samples participants using a random procedure so that the participants are representative of a population.

Rationale for mixed methods – This is a statement in a mixed methods study that advances the reason for collecting both quantitative and qualitative data and employing a mixed methods design. This reason should directly relate to the type of design (e.g., to compare the two databases in a convergent design, to explain the quantitative results in an explanatory sequential design, to explore in order to develop a quantitative instrument, intervention, or variables in an exploratory sequential design).

Sampling in mixed methods research – This set of procedures guides the researcher in selecting participants (and sites) in both quantitative and qualitative strands. The researcher employs particular sampling strategies within each of the mixed methods designs.

Saturation – Saturation is the point in data collection when the researcher has gathered data from several participants, and the collection of data from *new* participants does not add substantially to the codes or themes being developed.

Social justice design – This advanced design builds on one of the basic designs with the intent of studying a problem with an overall social justice framework (e.g., feminist or critical race theory) to improve the lives of individuals in society. The researcher threads this framework throughout the mixed methods study at different points, but it becomes a constant focus of the study.

Strand – This term refers to the qualitative or quantitative component of the study.

INDEX

SSAGE researchmethods

The essential online tool for researchers from the world's leading methods publisher

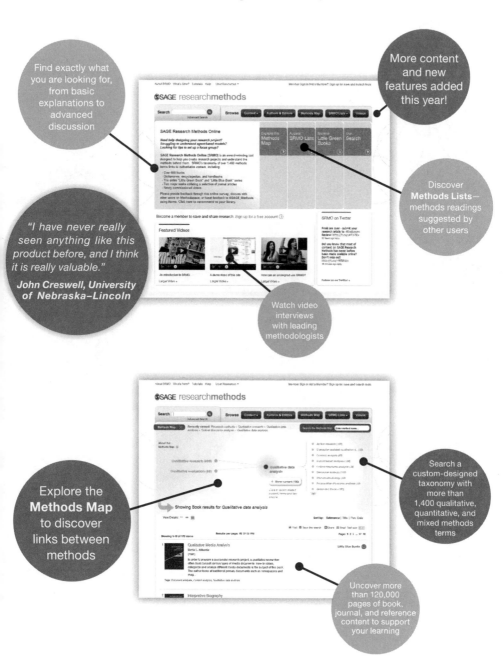

Find exactly what you are looking for, from basic explanations to advanced discussion

More content and new features added this year!

"I have never really seen anything like this product before, and I think it is really valuable."

John Creswell, University of Nebraska–Lincoln

Discover **Methods Lists**— methods readings suggested by other users

Watch video interviews with leading methodologists

Explore the **Methods Map** to discover links between methods

Search a custom-designed taxonomy with more than 1,400 qualitative, quantitative, and mixed methods terms

Uncover more than 120,000 pages of book, journal, and reference content to support your learning

Find out more at
www.sageresearchmethods.com